HARRY S. TRUMAN
The Man Who Walked With Giants

written and illustrated by
DAVID MELTON

Biographies and Footnotes by Teresa Marguerite Melton-Symon

D1404964

Richardson Printing, Inc.

RICHARDSON PRINTING
1490 Southern Road, Kansas City, MO 64120-1122

TO BESS TRUMAN
with admiration and respect

Library of Congress Cataloging in Publication Data
Melton, David.
  Harry S. Truman, the man who walked with giants.
  Bibliography: p.
  SUMMARY: A biography of the "common man" from Missouri
who became the 33rd President of the United States.
  1. Truman, Harry S., Pres. U.S., 1884-1972—Juvenile
literature. 2. Presidents—United States—Biography—Juvenile
literature. [1. Truman, Harry S., Pres. U.S.,
1884-1972. 2. Presidents] I. Title.
E814.M44   973.918'092'4 [B] [92]   80-22083
ISBN 0-8309-0293-7

Printed in the United States of America

TABLE OF CONTENTS

THE CHANGING OF PRESIDENTS

On April 12, 1945, a major news bulletin shocked the citizens of the United States.

**The President of the United States,
Franklin Delano Roosevelt, is dead!**

Upon hearing the news, drivers steered their cars to the sides of roads until they regained their composure.

Office workers sat in stunned silence.

Housewives stopped whatever they were doing and stood in disbelief.

As the news was received by members of the Armed Forces in Europe and in the South Pacific, American soldiers, sailors, and marines mourned the loss of their commander in chief.

With the realization that the President was dead, new questions were posed:

Who is the President now?

The Vice-President.

What's his name?

Truman.

What?

Harry Truman?

Where did **he** *come from?*

Missouri.

From where?

Harry S. Truman from Independence, Missouri.

Does he know enough to be President?

Who knows?

Throughout the country, news reporters began frantically searching for information about this man from Missouri who had been suddenly plummeted into the most influential office in the world. They learned that Harry S. Truman had been born on May 8, 1884, in Lamar, Missouri. His father, John Anderson Truman, and his mother, Martha Ellen Young Truman, were both descendants of pioneers who had immigrated to Missouri from Kentucky in the 1840s. He had one brother, John Vivian, and a sister, Mary Jane.

The American people quickly assumed that this man, Harry S. Truman, was no more than a common Midwest farmer. They feared that, at a time when our nation was engaged in an awesome world war against Germany in Europe and Japan in the Pacific, the leadership of our country had fallen on a man who was at best mediocre.

Harry S. Truman at six months of age.

JOHN ANDERSON TRUMAN — a shrewd livestock and cattle trader as well as a skillful farmer. Born on a farm in Jackson County, Missouri, in 1851, he died on November 5, 1914, following an operation.

MARTHA ELLEN YOUNG TRUMAN — majored in music and art at the Baptist Female College in Lexington, Missouri, before marrying Truman's father in 1881. She died on July 27, 1947, in Grandview, Missouri, at the age of eighty-four.

JOHN VIVIAN TRUMAN — younger brother of Harry Truman, born in 1886. He operated the Grandview, Missouri, farm until the age of twenty. For the next forty years, he was employed as a bank clerk in Kansas City. Following the close of World War II, he resumed his work as a farmer, cultivating the farm at Lamar, Missouri. He died on July 9, 1965.

MARY JANE TRUMAN — younger sister of Harry, born in 1889. Having a keen sense for farm management, she spent a great portion of her life on a farm. Along with her brother, John Vivian, she ran the Grandview, Missouri, farm until 1906. Never marrying, she took care of her elderly mother. Mary Jane died in 1978.

NO ORDINARY FARM BOY

In assessing the potentials of Harry Truman, the people of Independence, Missouri, had certain advantages. They knew him. They had seen him grow up. And they knew his family. They were well aware that, although his parents were of pioneer stock, they were far from ordinary or mediocre.

Harry's father, John Anderson Truman, was a hardworking farmer and a smart horse trader. He was a small, wiry, rough and tumble man, quick with words and sometimes quicker with his fists. He was a man who could be pushed just so far and then the person pushing had better prepare to fight or run for his life. One time when John Truman was a witness in a court case, the questioning lawyer made the mistake of pushing too far. When he suggested that John was not telling the truth, John jumped to his feet, doubled his fists, and chased the lawyer out of the courthouse. John Truman had a stern and sturdy code of honor. And he stressed those values to his children.

Nor was Harry's mother, Martha Ellen Young Truman, an ordinary farm woman. She was extremely well read and loved music. She taught Harry to read before he was five years old and instilled in him an appreciation for classical music. She gave him his first piano lessons. Later Mrs. Truman enrolled him for regular lessons with a pupil of the Viennese professor who had taught Paderewski and Rubenstein.

When Mrs. Truman learned that her son's eyesight was poor, she immediately purchased glasses for him. Because the doctor overemphasized the dangers of breaking the glasses, Mrs. Truman insisted that Harry not participate in baseball, football, and other sports.

Because of these restrictions, young Harry spent much of his time reading and became an avid student of world history. When he was nine years old, he suffered a severe attack of diphtheria and was paralyzed for a time. As he slowly recovered, he and the doctor's son, who was also interested in military history, constructed a miniature replica of the wooden bridge that Julius Caesar's legionnaires had built across the Rhine.

EARLY INTEREST IN POLITICS

In school, Harry was an excellent student. Although he wasn't allowed to participate in sports, he was well liked by the other students and he made many close friends. One was a pretty blue-eyed, golden-haired girl named Bess Wallace. "She was my first sweetheart," Truman said many years later. "Her eyes are still blue, but her hair is not golden—it's silver, like mine. And she is still my sweetheart."

Young Harry was vitally interested in his community and began keeping detailed records of animal husbandry and of crops planted by area farmers. He recorded major events in his diaries. Harry's love for making notes and keeping thorough records would last throughout his life.

Harry's mother and father were also extremely interested in both local and national politics. In 1900, when Harry was sixteen, the National Democratic Convention was held in Kansas City. John Truman, a staunch Democrat, attended every session and took Harry with him. The convention was dominated by William Jennings Bryan, an eloquent and bombastic speaker who fancied himself the "champion of the common man." Young Harry was fascinated by the excitement of cheering crowds and political debates.

In 1901, Harry graduated from high school. He hoped to be accepted at West Point or Annapolis and he spent extra time studying algebra and Latin in preparation for the entrance exams. His hopes were destroyed, however, when he was told at the army recruiting station in Kansas City that his poor eyesight would disqualify him.

When his father lost most of his money in a bad business investment, Harry's chances of attending any college ended, so he took a job as a timekeeper with a work gang on the Santa Fe Railroad. His salary was only $35 a month (plus room and board). He worked with hobos and migrant railroad workers. This job offered him "a very down-to-earth education in the handling of men." He later went to work for a Kansas City bank and was quickly promoted to more responsible jobs. Because of his interest in the theatre, Harry managed to see almost every theatrical production that came to town.

In 1905, Harry joined the National Guard, Battery B, a field artillery unit. He paid twenty-five cents a week for the privilege of drilling at the armory. Due to his interest in military history, he had a keen respect and liking for military rank and file.

BESS WALLACE TRUMAN – wife of President Truman. She was born on February 13, 1885, to the wealthy David Willock Wallaces. She died in Independence, Missouri, at the age of 97, on October 18, 1982.

LAMAR, MISSOURI — the county seat of Barton County located in the southwestern part of the state. The Truman children were born there in a house built by their father. The Truman farm later belonged to Everett Earp, a relative of the famous gunfighter Wyatt Earp. After World War II, John Vivian Truman (Harry's brother) became the owner of the farm. When he retired, the farm was designated a national historical landmark representing President Truman's birthplace.

GRANDVIEW, MISSOURI — situated in western Missouri just south of Kansas City. It became a city in 1929 and is now the site of several manufacturing firms which produce mounted hydraulic cranes, safety lights for heavy equipment, electric components for radios, and machine parts for small planes. In 1890, the Truman family moved from Lamar, Missouri, into a farmhouse constructed by Truman's grandfather, Solomon Young. They lived there for three years before moving to Independence, Missouri.

WORLD WAR I — a major European conflict, from 1914 to 1918, involving Germany, Austria-Hungary, and Italy against England, France, and Russia. The United States tried to remain neutral but numerous attacks upon American vessels by German submarines outraged United States citizens and forced President Woodrow Wilson to declare war on Germany in April of 1917. Eight months later, Germany finally surrendered to the Allies on November 11, 1918.

CAPTAIN HARRY OF BATTERY D

By the time the United States entered World War I in April of 1917, Harry had been out of the National Guard six years. He reenlisted and was elected lieutenant by the men in his unit. (At that time, guardsmen chose their own junior officers.) When thirty-three-year-old Lieutenant Harry Truman was sent to Fort Sill in Oklahoma for training, he soon proved himself to be an able artilleryman. He displayed an outstanding ability for leading men and an uncanny knack for calculating the range of guns.

When Harry learned his regiment was to be sent overseas, he took advantage of a twenty-four-hour pass in New York City to get three extra pairs of glasses. When he started to pay for them, the patriotic optometrist wouldn't accept any money from the young soldier. Although Harry always insisted on paying his own way, he was touched by the man's insistence and finally accepted the gifts.

Assigned to the 129th Field Artillery, Harry was promoted to captain after arriving in France, and soon was placed in command of Battery D. It was known as the "Dizzy D" because the men were such an unruly group and had caused previous commanders so much trouble. Captain Truman called the noncommissioned officers and his men together. "I didn't come over here to get along with you," he told them. "You've got to get along with me. If there are any of you who can't, speak up right now . . . ." The men were impressed with the Captain's bluntness and decided to get along with him.

Captain Truman led his men to the combat line located in the Vosges Mountains. This confrontation with the enemy would later be called the Battle of Who Run because the artillery fire caused such panic in the new recruits that they began to "scatter like partridges." However, acting decisively, Captain Truman got his men back together without losing a man. From then on, Battery D was a seasoned outfit.

Captain Harry Truman proved himself an outstanding leader under fire. He led his men through some of the war's worst fighting. In September of 1917, Battery D took part in the Allied offensive against the Germans at St.-Mihiel. In October, Truman and his men moved with the division to the Argonnes Forest and engaged in the largest battle American soldiers had ever fought. Finally, on November 11, 1918, Germany surrendered.

After returning home to the United States, Captain Harry Truman received an honorable discharge.

TWO NEW PARTNERSHIPS

Back home in Independence, Harry Truman returned to civilian life and began two new ventures. One succeeded but the other was doomed to failure.

On June 28, 1919, he and his childhood sweetheart, Bess Wallace, were married. They were both in their mid-thirties. Why their courtship lasted so long remains a mystery. Some people have thought that Bess's mother, who was wealthier and more socially prominent than the Trumans, may have withheld her approval of the marriage. Others say both Harry and Bess were very deliberate people who refused to rush into any venture. After taking a honeymoon trip to Chicago and Port Huron, Michigan, the couple returned to Independence and moved into the Wallace house on North Delaware. The marriage lasted the rest of his life.

Another partnership he entered into was not as successful. Deciding against farming, Harry and his army buddy, Eddie Jacobson, opened a men's clothing store in Kansas City, Missouri. For the first two years the shop did very well. But in 1921, when the agricultural recession struck the Midwest and farm prices dropped to an all-time low, many small businesses were ruined. The Truman and Jacobson Haberdashery was no exception. Their inventory shrank from $35,000 to less than $10,000.

Deeply in debt, they were forced to close the store in 1922. Both Truman and Jacobson tried to pay their creditors. Jacobson finally had to declare bankruptcy but Harry was able to hold out and eventually paid every dollar he owed. He decided not to go back into merchandising again, nor would he turn to farming. Instead, Harry Truman was about to embark upon a new career — politics.

INDEPENDENCE, MISSOURI — located to the immediate east of Kansas City. Founded in 1827, Independence was a very important city during the nineteenth century because it lay directly in the path of the Santa Fe and Oregon trails. Here members of wagon trains regrouped and gathered supplies before continuing their long journey westward. In 1846 the first mail stagecoach lines began at Independence, and during the Civil War, Union and Confederate forces fought bitterly in and around Independence. Confederate troops captured Independence twice but only for a few days each time. Independence is the county seat of Jackson County and its main products are chemicals, clothing, furniture, machinery, and plastic and metal products.

With Mrs. Truman.

"BOSS" PENDERGAST'S MACHINE

Harry Truman's parents were Democrats. His father had been a part-time member of the Democratic organization, and Harry became a Democrat too. In the spring of 1922, one faction of the Democratic Party (called "The Goats") was headed by Tom "Boss" Pendergast. They were looking for a strong candidate for county judge from the Eastern Division of Jackson County. Pendergast's nephew, Jim, had been an officer during World War I and had met Harry. Jim had heard about the clothing store closing, so he suggested the name of Harry Truman to his uncle.

Because of his interest in politics, Harry quickly agreed to run for the office. At that time, the county judge in Missouri was not a courtroom position. The county judges were more like county commissioners in other states who levied taxes, built and repaired county roads, maintained homes for the elderly and schools for delinquents and administered other county functions.

Harry soon learned that four other men were also seeking the nomination. Most of them had run for office before and had experience in getting votes. But Harry soon demonstrated he was a fast learner and quickly became a forceful opponent. Weighing down the back of his car with two cement bags so he wouldn't get stuck in the mud, Harry set out across the country roads to shake hands with farmers and businessmen in every town and precinct in the Eastern District of Jackson County. He enlisted votes from Army buddies, fellow members of the Masonic Lodge, and numerous relatives throughout the county.

On the day of the primary, Harry Truman won the nomination and three months later, the election. However, two years later, his opponents got even by throwing their support to the Republican candidate. Harry suffered his first and only defeat.

Finding himself out of work again, Harry took a job selling memberships in the Kansas City Automobile Club. He needed the money because, on February 17, 1924, he and Bess became the proud parents of a baby daughter, Margaret.

Besides working for the Auto Club, Harry also became an officer in a successful building and loan business. He did not stay with either of these ventures for long—he had been bitten by the political bug and was eager to run for office again. So, when the opportunity to run for presiding judge of Jackson County presented itself in 1926, Harry was ready and willing. With the support of "Boss" Pendergast and his powerful political machine, Truman won the election by more than 16,000 votes.

Throughout the campaign, Truman had vowed to run an honest, economical government. While many people believed such a promise impossible for a Pendergast candidate to keep, they figured that if anyone could do it, that man was Harry S. Truman. And he proved them right. When Pendergast's associates urged Truman to "play ball" in awarding their companies most of the construction contracts, he stubbornly refused unless they turned in the lowest bids for the jobs. While that irritated many men in the party, it amused "Boss" Pendergast and he delighted in telling them, "I told you he's the contrariest man in the state of Missouri."

By the time Truman's term of duty as presiding judge came to a close in 1934, he had proved himself an energetic and efficient administrator. He had refurbished the Independence Courthouse, improved all the county roads, and managed the finances so well that the county had a handsome surplus of funds.

KANSAS CITY, MISSOURI — second largest grain and livestock center in the United States. Founded in 1889, it was originally called "Westport Landing." Located at the intersection of the Kansas (Kaw) and Missouri rivers on the western border of Missouri, it is one of the two biggest cities in the state. Being one of the largest business and transportation crossroads in the nation, Kansas City is also known as "The Gateway to the Southwest."

THOMAS J. PENDERGAST — operator of one of the nation's largest political machines in Kansas City, Missouri, from 1925 to 1940. "Big Tom" Pendergast was known as a man of greed and corruption. He became involved in fixing elections resulting in government positions being filled by candidates of his choosing. Nevertheless, he did prove to be extremely charitable to the poor and, as owner of a major concrete company, he facilitated the construction of much needed civic buildings including the internationally famous Country Club Plaza with its paved Brush Creek.

MARGARET TRUMAN DANIEL – daughter of Harry S. Truman. A talented woman, she became a concert soprano, television actress, wife, mother and author of over twenty books. She passed away in Chicago, Illinois, at the age of 83, on January 29, 2008.

FROM PRECINCT TO SENATOR

Because of his outstanding work as a presiding judge, Harry Truman expected a chance to move up another step on the political ladder. But several problems confronted him. It was 1932 and the nation was in the midst of its worst economic depression. By spring, the people of a despairing country began to hear their first words of hope. Franklin Delano Roosevelt, the ex-governor of New York State, had begun his campaign for the Democratic presidential nomination. He eloquently promised a "New Deal" for the American people. Ready for a change, voters elected Roosevelt by a landslide.

As the nation attempted to recover from the Great Depression, the ill winds of scandal were brewing in Missouri. "Boss" Pendergast's connections with mobster chief Johnny Lazia made front page news headlines. When four people were killed by Lazia's hoodlums, Pendergast's reputation was damaged even further and, for the first time, his political machine had difficulty in finding a candidate to run for an opening in the U.S. Senate. The word was out—Pendergast was on his way down and no one wanted to be aboard his sinking ship. But "Boss" Pendergast thought he might find the needed candidate in Jackson County—Harry S. Truman.

When Pendergast sent two of his men to discuss the idea, some persuading was necessary before Harry agreed to run for office. His chances for winning weren't good. He wasn't well known outside of Jackson County and the support of Pendergast was bound to work against his campaigning. Making the prospect even worse, two veteran congressmen, John L. Cochran and Jacob L. Milligan, were also seeking the nomination. It would have been a good year for Harry Truman of Independence to stand back and wait for better days. But the slight chance of being a U.S. Senator was too much for Harry to resist. And besides, he loved the challenge of campaigning against such staggering odds.

Truman was already an avid supporter of Roosevelt's "New Deal" and he was also an eager and vigorous campaigner with a style all his own. Harry traveled in his automobile throughout Missouri. He often made as many as sixteen speeches a day in small towns and every wide place in the road where he could gather an audience of farmers or shopkeepers. His decision to aim his campaign toward the rural voters proved to be a wise one. He won the election by over 250,000 votes.

With Tom "Boss" Pendergast.

DEPRESSION OF THE 1930s — On October 24, 1929 (a day now referred to as "Black Thursday"), the stock market crashed, resulting in the economic instability of the United States. Banks closed, mortgages foreclosed, industrial productivity dwindled, and commerce all but stopped. Twelve million Americans were unemployed and impoverished. Many major businesses were forced into bankruptcy. President Hoover authorized the Reconstruction Finance Corporation, designed to rescue banks, businesses, and railroads from total collapse. But not until Franklin Delano Roosevelt became President of the United States in 1933 did the nation's economy begin to show signs of improvement.

With Margaret and Mrs. Truman.

THE SENATOR DEFIES THE ODDS

That winter, Harry and Bess Truman and their ten-year-old daughter Margaret moved to Washington, D.C. On January 3, 1935, thirteen new senators, all Democrats, were sworn into office and Harry S. Truman from Independence was one of them.

Senator Harry Truman was now fifty years old. He was an experienced combat veteran of a world war and he had successfully challenged the Missouri politicians. But in Washington he admitted he felt out of place and "as timid as a country boy." One seasoned Senator told him, "For the first six months, you'll wonder how you got here and, after that, you'll wonder how the rest of us got here."

Harry soon noticed that there seemed to be two kinds of senators. One group was extremely conscientious and hardworking while the other group got most of the publicity. It didn't take him long to decide which group he wanted to be in. He had come to Washington **to work**.

When President Roosevelt made his State of the Union Address proposing major reforms and introducing a long list of bills and resolutions in the Senate, Senator Truman carried an armload of papers home that evening and studied their contents late into the night. Working late soon became routine—and he loved it. "I was now where I belonged," he later said. Soon some of the other senators began to notice Truman's tireless work habits. After Truman offered a piece of information in the Senate, one of his leading Republican colleagues, Arthur H. Vandenberg, commented, "When the Senator from Missouri makes a statement like that, we can take it for the truth."

After six years of hard work, the Senator from Missouri was in trouble in his own state—Pendergast again! Tom Pendergast was indicted for accepting bribes from several of the nation's leading insurance companies in order to pay for his passion of betting on horses. Realizing that he was caught and too tired and sick to put up a fight, Pendergast pleaded guilty and was sent to jail for fifteen months.

Since another man had announced his intentions to run for Truman's Senate seat, it appeared that Truman didn't have a chance of winning. When President Roosevelt suggested that if Truman would withdraw from the race, he would offer him a job on the Interstate Commerce Commission, Truman was furious. He sent a note back to the White House informing the President that he had no intention of pulling out and that he intended to run even if he "only got one vote."

Harry returned to Missouri and started campaigning with his usual determination. With the help of his impressive voting record in the Senate and his unique straight-from-the-shoulder speaking, he beat the odds and won the election. When he returned to the Senate on January 3, 1941, his colleagues awarded him a standing ovation.

Truman proved he was not only a scrappy fighter—he was also a winner. Although the shadow of Tom Pendergast's corruption and scandal had not completely disappeared, it was beginning to fade. Harry Truman was establishing himself as a man of indisputable integrity and honor.

THE TRUMAN COMMITTEE

In 1941, with each passing day, the prospect of a second world war became more imminent. Under the leadership of Adolf Hitler, Germany was beginning to engulf neighboring countries. Europe was in flames. In Asia, Japanese forces invaded China, and there was cause to believe that war in the Pacific might soon erupt.

President Roosevelt called for enormous increases in the production of military weapons. Billions of dollars in contracts were awarded to construction companies for the purpose of building and expanding factories. When Senator Truman heard rumors that much of this money was being wasted and misspent in the construction of Fort Leonard Wood in Missouri, he proved himself a true son of the "Show Me" state and went there to see for himself. He soon learned that the charges were true.

In the days that followed, the Senator drove his car throughout the nation to observe army camp installations and factory and mill construction. Not only did he find evidence of extravagance and graft but he also found that too many contracts were going out to large companies without proper bidding practices. The idea that companies were engaged in such illegal practices at a time when our country was in a dangerous position sickened him.

Returning to Washington, D.C., Truman reported his findings. The Senate immediately responded by making Truman head of a special investigating committee. The Truman Committee moved quickly into action. Its members organized hearings and visited aircraft plants, shipyards, and other military installations. They found evidence of mismanagement on a tragic scale. They saw engines that didn't fit the planes for which they were being manufactured, a bomber whose wings were not long enough to insure stable flight, and a Quartermasters Corps that rented equipment rather than buying it — a practice which cost the government a needless thirteen million dollars.

Because of the Truman Committee findings, many reforms were forced upon the United States Army, Navy, and manufacturers. It has been estimated that the committee saved the taxpayers up to fifteen billion dollars and thousands of lives.

Within weeks after the committee was formed, its discoveries began making headlines. The name of Harry S. Truman was fast becoming a well recognized and highly respected name in Washington, D.C.

PEARL HARBOR — American naval base located on the Hawaiian island of Oahu. It gained historic renown when the Japanese attacked it early on Sunday morning, December 7, 1941. Their surprise aerial attack scuttled three American battleships as well as one minelayer and target ship; 174 American planes, four battleships, three cruisers, and three destroyers of the United States Naval Fleet received irreparable damage; 2,330 American sailors and soldiers were killed and 1,145 were wounded.

AMERICA GOES TO WAR

On December 7, 1941, the Japanese attacked Pearl Harbor. In his radio announcement to the American people, President Roosevelt described that day as one that "will live in infamy." A state of war was declared between the United States and the Japanese Empire.

Three days later on December 11, Germany and Italy declared war on the United States. While the two battle lines were divided by thousands of miles — the Japanese to the west in the South Pacific and the Germans and Italians eastward across the Atlantic Ocean in Europe — the people of the United States had never been more united in their courage and determination to win on both fronts.

When the Democratic Convention was scheduled to meet in Chicago in 1944, there was no doubt that Franklin Delano Roosevelt would be nominated for reelection to an unprecedented fourth term. President Roosevelt was more than willing to keep Vice-President Henry A. Wallace as his running mate, but many of the leaders of the Democratic Party were insistent on dropping Wallace from the ticket because they thought his liberal views would cost the party votes in the South. Reluctantly, Roosevelt finally agreed. But who would the candidate for Vice-President be?

As Senator Harry Truman, his wife Bess, and their daughter Margaret drove from Independence, Missouri, to Chicago, Illinois, they had no idea that the name of Truman was being mentioned throughout the leadership of the Democratic Party. Harry was looking forward to nominating Senator James F. Byrnes for the office. Little did he know that within a few days he would have to make one of the major decisions of his life.

After the Trumans arrived in Chicago, several delegates mentioned to Harry that he was being considered for the vice-presidential nomination. Truman didn't believe it and thought nothing more about it.

Following Roosevelt's expected nomination, Robert Hannegan, the chairman of the Democratic Committee, went to the Steven's Hotel to see Harry and told him that Roosevelt wanted him as the vice-presidential candidate. Harry Truman still couldn't believe it. He told Hannegan to thank the President for the consideration but to tell him that Harry Truman was very happy in the Senate and had no desire to be Vice-President.

SEARCHING FOR A VICE-PRESIDENT

The next day Hannegan called Truman and invited him to come to his suite at the Blackstone Hotel. When Harry arrived, Hannegan picked up the telephone and placed a long distance call to President Roosevelt who was in San Diego, California, at the time. When Roosevelt's booming voice answered, everyone in the hotel room could hear it.

"Bob, have you got that fellow lined up yet?" he wanted to know.

"No," Hannegan replied and then unknowingly repeated what Pendergast had said about Truman years before. "He's the contrariest Missouri mule I've ever dealt with!"

"Well," Roosevelt instructed, his voice growing even louder, "you tell him that if he wants to break up the Democratic Party in the middle of a war, that's his responsibility."

Truman later said, "I was, to put it mildly, stunned. I stood around for about five minutes and then I said, 'I'll do what the President wants.'"

On July 21, 1944, defeating Henry Wallace on the second ballot, Harry S. Truman won the Democratic nomination for Vice-President. Making his way through the roaring crowd, Harry walked to the platform and gave one of the shortest acceptance speeches on record. It was composed of ninety-two words:

> You don't know how very much I appreciate the very great honor which has come to the state of Missouri. It is also a great responsibility which I am perfectly willing to assume.
>
> Nine years and five months ago, I came to the Senate. I expect to continue the efforts I have made there to help shorten the war and to win the peace under the great leader, Franklin Delano Roosevelt.
>
> I don't know what else I can say except that I accept this great honor with all humility.
>
> I thank you.

After he finished, the crowd went wild with enthusiasm. The police had to form a protective circle around Harry, his wife, and their daughter to hold back the cheering delegates. When they finally got outside where a car was waiting, Bess turned to Harry and asked, "Are we going to have to go through this for all the rest of our lives?"

He didn't answer.

HENRY A. WALLACE — Vice-President from 1941 to 1945 under Franklin D. Roosevelt. Born in Adair County, Iowa, in 1888, he functioned as Secretary of Agriculture (1933-1940) and as Secretary of Commerce (1945-1946). In addition, Wallace was the Progressive Party's 1940 presidential nominee. Outside of his political career, he proved an expert in plant culture and developed a successful hybrid seed corn. Mr. Wallace died in 1966.

With President Roosevelt.

TRUMAN'S NEW CONCERNS

It wasn't until President Roosevelt returned from military conferences in Hawaii in mid-August that he and Harry met again to discuss campaign plans. The two had lunch outside on the White House grounds. During that meeting, they agreed that since Roosevelt needed to pay close attention to the war, the responsibility of traveling throughout the country to make campaign speeches would be left to Truman. There was little doubt that the assignment suited Harry Truman's talents. He had already proved himself to be a forceful orator and a crowd-pleaser.

After the meeting as Truman left the White House, waiting reporters inquired about Roosevelt's state of health. "He's still the leader he's always been," Truman quickly replied. "He's as keen as a briar."

The reporters accepted the answer but they weren't convinced. They suspected that Franklin Roosevelt's health problems were more serious than they had been told. In private, Truman was very concerned about the President's condition. The demands of office and the added pressure of the war had taken their toll on the commander in chief.

FRANKLIN DELANO ROOSEVELT — thirty-second President of the United States from 1933 to 1945. As this country's leader, he steadfastly guided its people through turbulent times. He maintained a sense of stability during the Depression of the 1930s by enforcing a series of emergency measures designed to strengthen the American economy, promote increases in agricultural and industrial production, and protect the ownership of homes as well as supply the unemployed with work. Throughout World War II, he actively dealt with the overall management of diplomatic affairs and in the determining of Allied objectives. By the beginning of his third term as President, he had firmly established himself as the vanguard of United States foreign policy and the standardbearer of American ideals. Roosevelt died in 1945, just three weeks before the German surrender.

THE SMEAR CAMPAIGN

A few weeks later, Eddie McKim, longtime friend and army buddy of Truman, attended a reception at the White House. He was shocked at President Roosevelt's unhealthy appearance. As he and Harry left, Mr. McKim stopped on the sidewalk, turned to his friend, and said, ". . . turn around and take a look. You're going to be living in that house before long."

For a moment, Harry stood quietly and looked at the building. "I'm afraid I am," he finally answered.

The mudslinging during the campaign was thick and heavy. The Republican candidate, Thomas E. Dewey, and the newspapers hesitated to openly criticize the President because they were afraid the voters might think such an approach unpatriotic. Instead, they began to attack Harry Truman. They repeatedly charged that anyone who had had dealings with Tom "Boss" Pendergast was crooked too. The Hearst newspaper unleashed the worst smear of all by circulating the rumor that Truman had once been a member of the Ku Klux Klan. But none of the attacks worked. On November 11, 1944, Roosevelt and Truman soundly defeated the Republican candidates, Dewey and Bricker, by more than 3.5 million votes.

DEMOCRATIC PARTY — stems from the earlier Anti-Federalist Party and was named by Thomas Jefferson. In 1828, Andrew Jackson was elected the first Democratic President of the United States.

REPUBLICAN PARTY — also known as "The Grand Old Party." It was firmly established in June of 1856 at the first Republican nominating convention in Philadelphia, Pennsylvania. In 1860, Abraham Lincoln became the first Republican President of the United States.

VICE-PRESIDENT TRUMAN

On January 20, 1945, while standing on the south portico of the White House, Henry Wallace, the retiring Vice-President, administered the oath of office to Harry S. Truman, the newly elected Vice-President. Flanked by a secret service man and his son, James, President Franklin Delano Roosevelt delivered his fourth inaugural address. He was almost sixty-three years old and looked gray and tired; nevertheless, he refused to wear an overcoat as he made his speech.

During the next eighty-two days, Harry Truman enjoyed his duties as Vice-President. He took over as presiding officer of the Senate and he and Mrs. Truman attended many of Washington's social functions. They filled in for the President at such times as when Roosevelt attended the meeting at Yalta with Winston Churchill, Great Britain's Prime Minister, and Josef Stalin, the Premier of Russia.

However, one invitation Truman regretted having accepted was to a National Press Club party. Some of the reporters who had heard that he played the piano asked if he would play for them. Truman cheerfully walked over to the piano and began to play. He had struck only a few notes when someone else urged screen actress Lauren Bacall to move in closer so a picture could be taken. Soon Miss Bacall was seated atop the piano striking a good-natured sultry pose for the photographers' cameras.

The scene was a publicity man's delight and the Vice-President's nightmare. Truman quickly realized he was in trouble but, afraid of hurting Miss Bacall's feelings, he was too polite to refuse more pictures. The next morning they were printed on the front pages of most of the newspapers in the country. Harry Truman feared the pictures would give the nation a false image of their Vice-President. Mrs. Truman agreed that they were in questionable taste and she thought they made her husband look undignified. Although there were some negative comments about the pictures, most people thought they showed that the serious-minded Vice-President from Missouri had a sense of humor.

YALTA CONFERENCE — a meeting in early February of 1945 between Roosevelt, Churchill, and Stalin at Yalta, a Russian city on the Crimean peninsula in the Black Sea. At this conference, paramount decisions were made about the postwar world. The three leaders agreed that, when Germany surrendered, the country and its capital, Berlin, would be divided into four sections, each occupied by an Allied power. Stalin also agreed that Russia would participate in the struggle against Japan within two to three months after the fall of Germany. In turn, Roosevelt and Churchill consented to allow the Russians to annex any Asian land lost during previous wars and the right to occupy part of Korea. It was also agreed that Poland and other liberated nations of Eastern Europe would receive financial aid and advisory help in forming new governments elected freely by their own peoples. Foremost in the conference, Roosevelt, Churchill, and Stalin developed a common strategy in securing world peace by agreeing to create an international peace organization which would become known as the United Nations.

"HE WAS MY FRIEND"

When Truman received word that Tom Pendergast had died on January 26, 1945, reporters wanted to know if he planned to attend the funeral in Kansas City, Missouri. To their surprise, Truman quickly answered, "Of course I am. He was always my friend and I have always been his."

Even those who questioned if openly admitting friendship with a convicted criminal was wise had to admire Truman's courage. Harry Truman attended the funeral and later wrote of Tom Pendergast:

> *In his prime, he was a clear thinker and understood political situations and how to handle them. His word was better than the contracts of most businessmen. His physical breakdown in 1936 got him in serious trouble.*
>
> *I never deserted him when he needed friends. Many for whom he'd done much more than he ever did for me ran out on him when the going got rough. I didn't do that ....*
>
> *Politics force men into contacts with all manners of people but men of principle need never surrender them in order to gain or to hold political office .... Several grand juries, both state and federal, went over my career as a county judge with a fine tooth comb and of course they could only give me a clean bill of health.*

Harry Truman insisted that Tom Pendergast never asked him to do anything dishonest because "he knew I wouldn't do it."

ELEANOR ROOSEVELT — wife of President Franklin Roosevelt. Born in 1884, she overcame her shy nature to fervently champion the causes of racial equality and the betterment of mankind. During World War II, she traveled thousands of perilous miles to visit embattled American troops and made many dangerous journeys to war-torn countries. At the war's end, she was appointed to the United Nations General Assembly as a delegate and participated in the drafting of the United Nations Declaration of Human Rights. Her concern for humanity earned her the title of "First Lady of the World." Mrs. Roosevelt died on November 7, 1963.

With Mrs. Roosevelt.

THE THIRTY-THIRD PRESIDENT

After returning from the Yalta Conference, President Roosevelt reported on his discussions with Churchill and Stalin to a joint session of Congress on March 1, 1945. Exhausted from the trip Roosevelt went to his Warm Springs, Georgia, home for a much needed rest.

On April 12, 1945, President Roosevelt suffered a cerebral hemorrhage and at 3:35 in the afternoon he died.

At that time, Harry Truman was presiding over proceedings in the Senate. It was almost two hours before he learned that events had just placed him in one of the most awesome offices in the world.

When the Senate adjourned at about five o'clock that evening, Truman stopped by the office of his good friend, Speaker of the House Sam Rayburn. As soon as he walked in, Rayburn told Truman that Steve Early, the President's press secretary, had telephoned and asked that Truman call him back at the White House as soon as possible.

Truman placed the call. When Early answered, his voice seemed strained.

"Please come right over," he said. "And come in through the main Pennsylvania Avenue entrance," he added.

Truman didn't suspect the real reason for the call. He figured that Roosevelt must have returned to Washington and wanted to discuss something with him. He was puzzled, however, by Early's instructions to use the main official entrance to the White House since Truman was accustomed to using the side entrance.

Going directly from Rayburn's office, Truman walked without his usual secret service man through the basement of the Capitol Building to his car. It was about 5:25 p.m. when he arrived at the White House. He was immediately escorted to Mrs. Roosevelt's study on the second floor. When he entered the room, he saw that Mrs. Roosevelt was not alone. Her daughter, Anna Roosevelt Boettiger; Anna's husband, Colonel John Boettiger; and Steve Early were there.

Seeing Truman, Mrs. Roosevelt said quite simply, "Harry, the President is dead."

Momentarily stunned, Truman stood silently trying to realize what he had just heard.

Finally, with concern for Mrs. Roosevelt, he said, "Is there anything I can do for you?"

Mrs. Roosevelt shook her head and replied, "Is there anything we can do for *you*? For you are the one in trouble now."

31

"...PRAY FOR ME"

After Mrs. Roosevelt left the room, Truman telephoned Chief Justice Harlan Stone to come to the White House as soon as possible. He sent his car for Bess and Margaret and then phoned both the leaders of the House of Representatives as well as the leaders of the Senate. At 7:00 p.m., Chief Justice Stone administered the oath of office to Harry S. Truman —*the thirty-third President of the United States of America.*

It was a somber occasion. Those present forced back tears of grief over Roosevelt's death.

Following the swearing in, Harry Truman performed his first function as President by calling a meeting of Roosevelt's Cabinet. He assured its members that he wanted them to stay in office. Then he made his first presidential decision —the San Francisco Conference, at which the United Nations Charter was to be drafted, would proceed as scheduled by the late President Roosevelt.

After the meeting ended, President Truman took his wife and daughter home to their apartment at 4701 Connecticut Avenue.

The following day, as reporters crowded around to get a few words from the new President, Truman suddenly turned toward them.

"I don't know if you fellows ever had a load of hay or a bull fall on you," he said simply, "but last night the moon, the stars, and all the planets fell on me. If you fellows ever pray, pray for me."

Surprised by his statement and touched by his seriousness, the reporters grew quiet. They must have wondered how such a simple man could ever be President.

The death of Franklin Roosevelt plunged the nation into a period of mourning. On the morning of April 14, a flag-draped coffin was carried on a horse-drawn caisson through the streets of Washington, D.C. Thousands of people lined the route to pay their last respects to their fallen leader —many wept openly. After a simple funeral at the White House, the cortege escorted the President's body to Hyde Park, New York, for burial.

With Mrs. Truman.

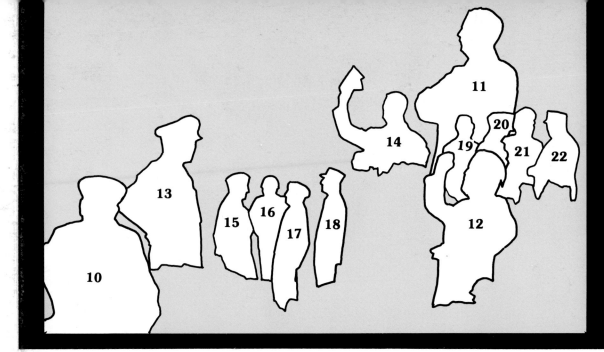

10. **JOSEF STALIN** — Premier of Russia

11. **ADOLF HITLER** — Chancellor of Germany

12. **BENITO MUSSOLINI** — Dictator of Italy

13. **GENERAL DWIGHT D. EISENHOWER** — Supreme Commander of Allied Expeditionary Forces in Europe

14. **NEVILLE CHAMBERLAIN** — Prime Minister of Great Britain (from 1937 to 1940)

15. **GENERAL GEORGE S. PATTON** — Commander of Second U.S. Army Corps in charge of 75h, 8th and 3rd Armies

16. **GENERAL OMAR BRADLEY** — Leader of 12th U.S. Army Group

17. **FIELD MARSHAL BERNARD MONTGOMERY** — Commander of British 3rd and 8th Armies

18. **GENERAL CHARLES DE GAULLE** — Leader of Free French Forces

19. **RUDOLF HESS** — Secretary & Deputy to Hitler

20. **DR. JOSEPH GOEBBELS** — German Minister of Popular Enlightenment and Propaganda

21. **HEINRICH HIMMLER** — Head of Gestapo (German Secret Police), Minister of the Interior and Minister of Home Defense

22. **HERMANN GOERING** — Commander of Luftwaffe (German Air Force)

THE GIANTS OF WORLD WAR II

1. **FRANKLIN DELANO ROOSEVELT** — President of the United States

2. **WINSTON CHURCHILL** — Prime Minister of Great Britain

3. **HIROHITO** — Emperor of Japan

4. **HIDEKI TOJO** — Premier of Japan and Minister of War

5. **CHIANG KAI-SHEK** — Head of China's Nationalist Forces

6. **MAO TSE-TUNG** — Head of China's Communist Forces

7. **GENERAL DOUGLAS MacARTHUR** — Supreme Commander of Allied Forces in the Southwest Pacific

8. **ADMIRAL WILLIAM F. HALSEY** — Commander of U.S. Navy Third Fleet in the South Pacific

9. **FLEET ADMIRAL CHESTER W. NIMITZ** — Commander in Chief of U.S. Pacific Navy Fleet and Pacific Ocean Areas

WORLD WAR II — THE CAUSES AND THE EFFECTS

When Harry S. Truman took the oath of office, without fanfare or applause of cheering crowds, he quietly stepped into a world of giants.

The names of those giants were world renowned — HITLER, MUSSOLINI, CHURCHILL, HIROHITO, TOJO, MAC ARTHUR AND EISENHOWER.

To make his challenge even more awesome, Truman had to take over the job of perhaps the most flamboyant giant of them all — FRANKLIN DELANO ROOSEVELT.

The war fused together likely and unlikely allies against a ruthless assortment of enemies. Not only was the war clearly defined in territorial terms of geography and nations but it was also well defined in moral terms of right and wrong.

In 1917, Germany accepted full responsibility for World War I and agreed to the surrender conditions outlined in the Treaty of Versailles. The defeated Germany was expected to pay enormous reparations to the victorious Allies. Germany's colonies, overseas investments, and industries were shattered, and national pride sank to the lowest ebb. The financial depression of 1929 added another blow to the destitute country.

When Adolf Hitler arrived on the political scene in Germany, he promised a new and powerful Germany where everyone would prosper. Such promises received enthusiastic response, and in 1933, Hitler became Chancellor of Germany.

Adolf Hitler had dreams of ruling not only Germany but all of Europe as well. He firmly believed the German Aryan race (blond-haired, blue-eyed, and non-Jewish) was superior to all other peoples and felt that Germany was destined to surpass other nations in government, culture, and military might.

In 1936, Germany, Italy, and Japan withdrew from the League of Nations. Under the leadership of Benito Mussolini, Italy had just conquered Ethiopia in North Africa. Japan had successfully captured Manchuria, a region in Northeast China. In 1940, Germany, Italy, and Japan signed the Axis Pact (also known as the Rome-Berlin-Tokyo Axis) thus uniting in the pursuit of territorial expansion and world dominance.

Feeling that Germany had indeed been treated too harshly following World War I, Britain and France allowed Hitler to annex Austria in 1938 and, under the Munich Agreement, Great Britain allowed Germany to reclaim the Sudetenland from Czechoslovakia.

Although Hitler declared that Germany's repossession of the Sudentenland was "the last territorial claim I have to make on Europe," his statement was far from true. His insatiable desire for more *Lebensraum* (living space) kept increasing. Breaking all previous agreements, on September 3, 1939, Hitler ordered his gray-clad armed forces to invade the flat plains of Poland

ADOLF HITLER — leader of Germany from 1933 to 1945. He rose to power through the National Socialist German Workers Party, a political group he founded. As Chancellor of Germany, he molded and twisted the government into a dictatorship. His desire for world power led to World War II and his policies brought untold suffering and death to countless millions. However, he failed to achieve world dominance because Germany was defeated in 1945. It is believed that Hitler committed suicide in a Berlin air raid shelter just minutes before Allied Russian forces captured Berlin, the capital of Germany. He died at the age of fifty-six.

BENITO MUSSOLINI — Fascist Dictator of Italy from 1922 to 1943. Born in 1883 in the Italian village of Dovia, he was the son of the village schoolmistress and a blacksmith. A keen admirer of Adolf Hitler's ideas, Mussolini wished to expand Italy's territorial possessions. In 1936, his forces conquered the peaceful African nation of Ethiopia whose people, armed only with bows and arrows, were no match for machine guns. In 1939, Italy annexed Albania. However, Mussolini's promises to bring back the "glory that was Rome" were short-lived. In 1943 during World War II, the Allies invaded Italy and Italian partisans, who believed Mussolini had deceived their country, imprisoned him. When Hitler learned of Mussolini's fate, he ordered a group of specially trained paratroopers to rescue the fallen dictator. The mission was a success. His rescuers took him to the city of Milan where he became the leader of a puppet government. But toward the end of 1945 when German military might was crumbling. Mussolini was recaptured by Italian partisans and executed. His body was hung upside down on a meat hook and left to be mutilated by embittered Italian citizens.

Hitler's German Army spread across the continent of Europe like a cancerous growth. The German aggressors overthrew the governments of Poland, Denmark, Belgium, Luxembourg, the Netherlands, and, finally, France. Rumania, Hungary, Bulgaria, Yugoslavia, Czechoslovakia and Greece also fell victim to Hitler's war machine.

In 1940, England, France, Russia, and China joined forces to combat Germany, Italy, and Japan. The United States was not directly active in the struggle, but it had been supporting the Allies with desperately needed weapons, ammunition, and medical supplies.

Even though Japan was allied with Germany and Italy, its leaders rarely conferred with Hitler or Mussolini. Japan was a country of islands with only a few natural resources. Following World War I, it was becoming increasingly difficult for Japan to compete with other nations, such as the United States and Great Britain, in raw materials and colonies and on the international trade market.

Therefore, high-ranking Japanese militants ignored the personal views of their Emperor Hirohito and sent armies to conquer lands in Asia and the Pacific Ocean. In 1931, the Japanese invaded Manchuria which was also under attack by China. In 1937, the Japanese declared war on China. During the next four years nearly all of Asia and the Pacific fell subject to the Japanese expansion. Then on December 7, 1941, the Japanese bombed Pearl Harbor, an American naval base in the Pacific, and the United States entered the war with the Allies.

By late 1943, the Allies gained the upper hand in both the European and Pacific theatres. Slashing through German military forces in North Africa, the Allies concentrated their efforts toward conquering Nazi-occupied Italy. On D-Day, June 6, 1944, on the Normandy beaches of northwestern France, the Allied forces launched the largest amphibious assault in military history. The American, British, and French soldiers who took part in this major offensive brought with them the hope of freeing Europe from its German oppressors.

As the United States, English, and French forces advanced toward Germany from the west, the Russian allies moved their army inward from the east. In the winter of 1944, Hitler made one last desperate attempt to regain his iron hold on Europe by unleashing a final major German counterattack in the Ardennes region of Belgium. This conflict, known as the Battle of the Bulge, directly preceded the final collapse of Hitler's Third Reich.

In the South Pacific, battles on islands bearing strange names such as Midway, Guadalcanal, Iwo Jima, and Okinawa made front page news. These island battles were fierce and extremely costly in human lives. And even though the Allies were winning one victory after another, the Japanese stubbornly refused to consider the idea of surrender.

NEVILLE CHAMBERLAIN — member of Britain's Conservative Party and Prime Minister of Great Britain between 1937 and 1940. He adopted an appeasement policy just prior to World War II in hopes of securing peace in Europe. He played a major role in the Munich Agreement of 1939 which permitted Adolf Hitler to annex the Czechoslovakian Sudetenland. However, Hitler shunned all former diplomacy when his German forces invaded Poland in September of 1939. This offensive act compelled England and its ally, France, to declare war on Germany. Harshly criticized for his unsuccessful foreign policy and for the 1940 British defeat by German forces in Norway, Chamberlain chose to resign from office. Shortly after, he became ill and died.

HIROHITO — Emperor of Japan from 1926 to 1945. Born in 1901, Hirohito served as the 124th ruler in a line dating back centuries to Japan's earliest days. When he first became his country's ruler, he had gained control of a nation which was trying to become a democratic state. However, military extremists sought a far more powerful Japan. Hirohito personally opposed the militarism of the 1930s but his closet advisers persuaded him to keep his opinions silent for fear that the monarchy might be dissolved. He was allowed to remain a figurehead after Japan was defeated in 1945. He died at 88 years of age on January 7, 1989.

HIDEKI TOJO — Japanese Premier and Minister of War during World War II. The son of a general, Tojo was born in 1884. His background, training, and interests were mainly military. He belonged to a group of militarists who deplored democratic developments in Japan. He led his country into World War II against the United States and other Allied powers. As the tide of war turned against Japan, Tojo resigned. Arrested by triumphant American forces in 1945, he attempted suicide but failed. He was convicted of war crimes and hung on December 23, 1948.

TRUMAN — THE UNKNOWN

No new President had ever before taken office during a period of such widespread international crisis. As the war in Europe drew to a close, it left in its wake bomb-shattered cities, battle-scarred farmlands, and a mass of homeless people in dire need of medical facilities and food.

Russia's leader, Josef Stalin, was beginning to defy agreements by installing Communist governments in reconquered areas of Eastern Europe.

The completion of the war with Japan appeared to be at least a year and a half away and could cost the lives of hundreds of thousands of American soldiers.

The people of the United States, tired of wartime restrictions, were beginning to grow restless and uneasy about what would happen to the economy once the war did end. Having experienced economic recessions and a major depression following World War I, the doomsday criers were making grim predictions. The loss of their magnetic and forceful leader, FDR, made matters even worse.

This man Harry Truman who had become President was of unknown quality. Newspaper reporters all but ignored his past achievements and daily emphasized that he was no more than average. The leaders of the Allied nations, who had learned to respect the dynamic leadership of Roosevelt, had grave doubts about Truman's untried abilities in international affairs. Even Truman's own colleagues in the Senate and House of Representatives, who should have known better, were concerned that he might have been given a job he wasn't equipped to handle.

If Harry Truman had any doubts about himself, he rarely showed it. He took on the Presidency the same way he had taken on other jobs before. He jumped straight into the middle of the challenges with an all-out zeal not only to endure but to succeed.

He immediately began conferring with his Cabinet officers and members of the House and Senate. To familiarize himself with the details of the major issues at hand in both the United States and abroad, he spoke with military experts and diplomatic advisers. His days were filled with reading volumes of reports that informed him of complications in managing a wartime government. At night, fighting back fatigue, he carried home stacks of papers to read and analyze.

CONFRONTING THE ISSUES

During this time, President Truman made his first speech to a joint session of Congress. He promised to carry out Roosevelt's programs and agreements to the letter. Although the members of both the House and Senate cheered his declaration and promised their support, in private they tended to shake their heads and say, "Poor Harry."

He held his first press conference. The reporters, who were used to Roosevelt's masterful way with words and his ability to gracefully sidestep unwanted questions, didn't know what to make of Harry Truman's straightforward manner and blunt responses. They wondered if the new President really meant to be so forthright or if he simply wasn't bright enough to disguise his opinions and motives.

Josef Stalin, the Russian leader, underestimated Truman. He immediately took advantage of the situation by trying to acquire additional lands and to assert more influence over the control of Europe.

But Harry Truman quickly demonstrated that he was not easily manipulated. At his initial meeting with Vyacheslav Molotov, the Russian Foreign Minister, Truman gave the Russians their first taste of his frank disdain for anyone's attempt to hedge on an agreement. In no uncertain terms, he bluntly denounced Russia's devious tactics.

"I have never been talked to like that in my life!" the surprised Molotov exclaimed.

"Carry out your agreements," President Truman acidly replied, "and you won't get talked to like that!"

The Russian Foreign Minister began to suspect that this new President wasn't as mediocre as everyone had assumed and that he might well become a viable force.

In a special briefing, Secretary of War Henry Stimson gave the President more information about the "Manhattan Project."

"Within four months," Stimson predicted, "we shall, in all probability, have developed the most terrible weapon ever known in human history, one bomb which could destroy an entire city."

VICTORY IN EUROPE

The war in Europe was rapidly coming to an end. Realizing that defeat was inevitable, Adolf Hitler committed suicide on May 1, 1945. The following day, Allied Russian forces captured Berlin, the capital city of Germany, and German troops in Italy surrendered. On May 4, the German forces in the Netherlands, Denmark, and Northwest Germany surrendered.

On May 7, in the Allied headquarters at Reims, France, German Colonel General Alfred Jodl signed the documents of unconditional surrender of all German forces. That same evening the family of Harry S. Truman moved into the White House. Their new address was 1600 Pennsylvania Avenue — the home of the President of the United States.

At a special press conference and radio broadcast on May 8, President Truman announced to the people of the United States that the war in Europe had been won.

A joyful America celebrated. In cities and towns throughout the country, people gathered in the streets cheering, waving their arms, and dancing. President Truman felt jubilant too, but at the same time he was saddened. He wished that the cheers on V-E Day could have been heard by Franklin Roosevelt, who had died only twenty-seven days before the victory.

The joy of V-E Day was also marred by Harry Truman's first mistake as President. Ironically, that very morning, in a letter to his mother and sister, he wrote:

Never a day has gone by that some momentous decision didn't have to be made. So far, luck has been with me....I hope when the mistake comes, it will not be too great to remedy.

Only hours later, Foreign Economic Administrator Leo T. Crowley and Acting Secretary of State Joseph C. Crew came to Truman's office with an order that Roosevelt had approved but had not signed. Without reading the paper, Truman picked up a pen and signed it. The order authorized a cutback in the Lend Lease program to Great Britain, Russia, and our other allies. Although the war was over, those supplies were desperately needed and should not have been stopped. As soon as Truman realized what had happened, he retracted the order and wrote himself a strong note:

Never sign anything without reading it!

BIRTH OF THE UNITED NATIONS

In the spring of 1945, eight hundred delegates from forty-six nations met in San Francisco to create a charter for a new international organization — the United Nations.

During the weeks of meetings, the proceedings were slowed down again and again by Russia's lack of cooperation. Fearing that the United Nations might be doomed to failure, Truman sent his right-hand man, Harry Hopkins, to Moscow to reason with Josef Stalin. It proved to be a smart move. Stalin soon instructed Russia's representative to be more cooperative.

On June 26, President Truman addressed the final session of the United Nations Charter Conference:

> *The United Nations was born out of the agony of war . . . . We who work to carry out its great principles should always remember that this organization owes its existence to the blood and sacrifice of millions of men and women. It is built out of their hopes for peace and justice.*

THE POTSDAM CHALLENGE

One of the biggest challenges to President Truman's establishing himself as a world leader was about to take place—the Potsdam Conference.

When the war ended in Europe, Truman and Churchill agreed that a face-to-face meeting with Josef Stalin was necessary. Many problems concerning how the defeated Germany would be governed and reconstructed needed to be resolved. The Russians were hedging on their previous agreement which would have allowed the establishment of Poland as an independent country. Stalin consented to attend the meeting and chose Potsdam, a suburb of Berlin, as the place it should be held.

When Truman went to Potsdam, he fully realized that his position for effective bargaining wasn't as strong as it might have been. Several factors weakened it. He did not have a track record for negotiating on the international scene. Both Stalin and Churchill tended to believe the newspapers' opinions which repeatedly portrayed Truman as a man of average abilities.

Winston Churchill, prime minister of Great Britain, was afraid that Truman didn't understand the amount of control Russia was trying to gain over Eastern Europe. He began to urge Truman to bend some of the agreements which Roosevelt had made with Stalin.

He faced another problem. Roosevelt, either due to his ill health during the Yalta Conference or his urgent belief that the United States would need Russia's support in concluding the war with Japan, had made several unwise concessions to Stalin's demands.

Making matters worse, British elections were scheduled midway through the meetings. To Truman and Stalin's surprise (and probably Churchill's too), the gallant wartime leader's Conservative Party lost the election. England's new Prime Minister, Clement Attlee (another unknown), replaced Churchill at the conference.

For Harry Truman, Potsdam was an exhausting and exasperating experience. Both Churchill and Stalin preferred to start meetings late in the day. Although Truman, an early riser, preferred morning meetings, he was outvoted. He admired and immediately liked Churchill, but he discovered that the Prime Minister made extremely long speeches at the drop of a hat. He found Stalin obstinate, demanding, and often rude. Truman might have been tempted to react as had his father to the lawyer years before. He would probably have enjoyed doubling his fists and running the Premier of Russia out of the building.

Although at first Churchill cautiously observed Truman, he quickly grew to recognize the President's sharp-witted diplomacy and Stalin began to realize his perseverence.

UNITED NATIONS — headquarters situated in New York City, New York. The United Nations has six branches: The Security Council performs the major duty of preventing wars; the General Assembly discovers peaceful settlements to disputes and provides a forum where all nations are represented equally; the Economic and Social Council studies the social, economic, cultural, and health problems of the world; the International Court of Justice decides legal disputes; the Secretariat administers the work of the United Nations; and the Trusteeship Council looks after the welfare of persons living in colonial areas.

POTSDAM CONFERENCE — a meeting between President Truman, Premier Stalin, and Prime Minister Churchill who was replaced early on in the conference by a recently elected Clement Attlee. Taking place from July 17 to August 2, 1945, it was held in Potsdam, East Germany, a town located sixteen miles southwest of Berlin. They assembled to reconfirm the Yalta Conference plans concerning the control and occupation of Germany. They concluded that Germany's power potential should be neutralized through demilitarization and decartelization and that trials for war criminals should begin promptly.

With Winston Churchill.

"BIG BROTHER" AND "LITTLE BOY"

Several days after the Potsdam Conference began, Truman received an unusual telegram. It read:

TOP SECRET
PRIORITY
WAR 33556
TO SECRETARY OF WAR FROM HARRISON. DOCTOR HAS JUST RETURNED MOST ENTHUSIASTIC AND CONFIDENT THAT THE LITTLE BOY IS AS HUSKY AS HIS BIG BROTHER. THE LIGHT IN HIS EYES DISCERNIBLE FROM HERE TO HIGHHOLD AND I COULD HAVE HEARD HIS SCREAMS FROM HERE TO MY FARM.

Truman understood the code words — *Big Brother* was the Atomic Bomb One. *Little Boy* was Atomic Bomb Two. And the distance *from here to my farm* meant the noise was heard forty miles away.

A few days later, in a more complete report, President Truman was informed that the monster weapon was ready for use against Japan and waited only for his command. When the President mentioned the readiness of the weapon to Churchill and Stalin, both Truman and Churchill thought the Russian Premier's casual reaction meant he didn't really understand how powerful the weapon was. But

SIR WINSTON CHURCHILL — Prime Minister of England during World War II and from 1951 to 1955. Born in 1874, he held five important government positions throughout his illustrious political career. In his most famous role as Prime Minister during World War II, he managed his country's policies well and earned world renown for his strategic expertise and statesmanship. He assisted in the overall drafting and planning of the war. After the war, he supported the reconstruction of Europe under the Marshall Plan, warned the world of Soviet Communist aggression, and advocated the formation of NATO. He received a Nobel Prize for Literature for his six-volume work, *The Second World War.* Upon retirement in 1955, he was knighted by Queen Elizabeth II. He died in 1965 and was given a hero's farewell by his countrymen and compatriots throughout the world.

CLEMENT ATTLEE — Prime Minister of Great Britain from 1945 to 1951. Born in 1883, he also served as Lord of the Privy Seal from 1940 to 1942 and as Deputy Prime Minister from 1942 until 1945. As Prime Minister and a leader of the Labor Party, he began the policy of nationalizing England's principal industries and economic institutions. His policies resulted in the formation of the Bank of England, the beginning of public utilities, and the nationalization of both steel and coal it was later learned that, through a network of spies, Stalin probably knew as much about the development of the atomic bomb as they did. Although there was little discussion, both Churchill and Stalin agreed that the weapon should be used.

PACKAGE PROPOSAL FOR STALIN

Realizing that the meetings were becoming bogged down over minor issues, President Truman prepared a package proposal for Stalin which would allow a new Polish border, a readmittance of Italy into the family of nations, and a great reduction in the amount of reparation payments demanded from the defeated Germany. Stalin was so completely surprised by Truman's approach that he found himself agreeing to the terms.

Publicly, the meetings ended on a note of unity. Privately, Harry Truman knew the "Soviet Bear" wanted more than its lion's share of territory and more political dominance over other countries. Truman realized that Russia was bound to pose additional problems to world peace. And in the near future, Truman would have to face those problems.

But first, the war in the Pacific demanded his full attention. The Japanese must be defeated!

industries. In addition, the National Health Service was created, India finally obtained its independence, and the overall dismantling of the British Empire began. Internal difficulties and involvement in the Korean War brought about the defeat of the Clement Attlee Labor Ministry. In 1951, Sir Winston Churchill succeeded him as Prime Minister. Attlee died in 1967.

JOSEF STALIN — born Iosif Vissarionovich Dzhugashvili in 1879. He was the son of a shoemaker in the southern Russian province of Georgia. Between 1902 and 1917, he fell subject to numerous arrests and exilings to Siberia for his political views. During World War I, he joined Vladimir Lenin's Communist Bolshevik faction and chose as his revolutionary name, "Stalin," meaning "Man of Steel." Following the Bolshevik victory over the Russian Czar in 1917, Stalin ruthlessly maneuvered his way to power until he controlled both the Communist Party and the Russian government. No party member, government official, or Russian citizen was safe from exile to a labor camp or even execution should they oppose Stalin. As dictator, he initiated a series of "Five-Year Plans" to radically expand Russia's industries and, with the use of farm machinery, he modernized Russian agriculture. Following a paralytic stroke, Stalin died on March 5, 1953.

With Josef Stalin.

THE CONTROVERSIAL DECISION

The Japanese showed no signs of being willing to consider surrender and were determined to fight to the last man. American military chiefs estimated that an invasion of the Japanese mainland would cost between 500,000 and one million casualties and the deaths of over 175,000 American servicemen (twice the number of men that had been killed in Europe). There was no way to estimate how many Japanese soldiers and civilians would be killed. President Harry Truman felt he had no choice but to order the use of the atomic bomb against Japan.

Before giving that order, President Truman issued an ultimatum to the Japanese demanding their surrender. Millions of leaflets were dropped from American planes over the cities of Japan urging the people to insist that the government admit defeat. The official Japanese warlords responded, "Absurd."

At 9:15 Japanese time on the morning of August 6, 1945, the first atomic bomb struck the city of Hiroshima. The bomb was small by later standards but it contained an explosive force equal to twenty thousand tons of TNT. It destroyed the entire city, injuring and killing at least 75,000 Japanese.

While traveling home from the Potsdam Conference aboard the cruiser U.S.S. *Augusta,* the President received word that the mission of the B-29 Bomber *Enola Gay* had been accomplished.

Again, the President sent a message requesting that the Japanese surrender and millions more of the leaflets were dropped. The Japanese still refused to comply.

Three days later a second atom bomb was dropped on Nagasaki, injuring and killing an additional 35,000 Japanese. This convinced the Japanese that the destruction of the first explosion had not been a fluke. The United States did indeed have a devastating weapon at its command. Five days later the leaders of Japan accepted the Allied terms of an unconditional surrender.

The surrender ceremony was extremely impressive. President Truman chose the location. The signing took place in Tokyo Bay on the deck of the new battleship U.S.S. *Missouri.*

JAPAN SURRENDERS

President Truman listened attentively to the radio account of the proceedings which was broadcast around the world. Acting in his role as the Supreme Commander of Allied Forces in the Southwest Pacific, General Douglas MacArthur accepted the surrender of Japan. Immediately following the ceremony, radio transmission was switched to the White House where President Truman proclaimed the following day, September 2, 1945, to be V-J Day (Victory in Japan Day).

The war was over. For the first time in four years American soldiers were no longer fighting on foreign soil. Harry S. Truman had been President only four short months. Since the birth of our nation, no four-month period has been so crowded with history-making events.

The awesome destruction caused by the atomic bombs spawned numerous arguments about whether or not President Truman was right in ordering their use. Truman never faltered in his defense of that decision and said he never regretted it "for one minute. My chief purpose," he maintained, "was to end the war in victory with the least possible loss of American lives. I never had any qualms about using an instrument that finally ended the war..." and thereby saved the lives of hundreds of thousands of American soldiers and thousands of Japanese as well.

ATOMIC BOMB — tested on July 16, 1945, by American scientists at Alamogordo, New Mexico. It was first used as a weapon during World War II in a successful attempt to force the Japanese to surrender. Deriving from a single type of uranium, it has an explosive power equal to 20,000 tons of dynamite. Its immensely destructive potential has now been harnessed in the development of nuclear warheads, artillery shells, land mines, bazookas and torpedoes. The atomic bomb, however, has now become obsolete since far more powerful nuclear weapons have been invented.

OCCUPATION OF JAPAN — began in August of 1945 directly following the end of World War II. Appointed Supreme Commander of Japan, General Douglas MacArthur started by expediting the trials of twenty-eight major Japanese war criminals. In 1946, he initiated Japan's first free election and helped in the development of a new democratic constitution. The executive powers of the Emperor were abolished, Japanese women acquired the right to vote, and large estates were divided among poor farmers. On April 28, 1952, the United States occupation of Japan ended.

COMBATTING THE GIANTS AT HOME

Now that the wars in Europe and the South Pacific were over, President Truman realized that other battles were about to be waged within the United States itself. But these confrontations would not be fought with cannons and bazookas — they would be fought with heated arguments and organized strikes.

Wage and price controls had been set during the war by the federal government. Eager to resume peacetime profits, labor union leaders began to demand increased wages. Businessmen wanted to be allowed to raise prices on products.

Having seen firsthand the staggering rise of inflation which resulted in a severe recession following World War I, President Truman realized that converting the nation's industries from manufacturing war machinery to producing peacetime products could wreck the nation's economy. To avoid economic disaster, Truman did everything within his power to make the transition from a wartime economy to a peacetime economy as smooth as possible.

Only eighteen days after Truman had taken office, the coal miners' union leader, John L. Lewis, ordered his men to stop working until their wages were increased. Using his wartime powers, Truman reacted immediately by placing the mines under governmental control and ordered the men back to work. They had to comply.

But Lewis was not easily defeated. He was determined to try again. And he did. In 1946, Lewis called two more strikes. In 1949 and 1950, when Lewis again ordered his men out of the mines, Truman invoked the Taft-Hartley Act to insure continuation of the nation's coal supply.

Refusing to allow strikes to endanger American productivity and economy, during the next six years President Truman combatted similar efforts by United Steel and railroad workers.

Many union men believed Truman was against the labor unions. Nothing could have been further from the truth. He understood that aggressive moves to increase their wages were natural acts. Coming from a family of working people, he sympathized with labor's cause. However, he felt his first duty was to preserve the nation's economy. He revealed, in no uncertain terms, that the man from Missouri had the courage to challenge powerful unions.

During such confrontations, the news media and the American public were often shocked by Truman's salty language. He never hesitated in calling a spade a spade or a damn a damn. Although most people were accustomed to hearing such words at work or on the streets, they had never heard a President of the United States unleash them publicly. Even though his vocabulary was often criticized, Truman refused to curb his blunt remarks or temper his choice of words. While his salty language offended some people, others rather admired his unpretentious candor and directness.

JOHN L. LEWIS — President of the United Mine Workers from 1920 to 1960 and founder of the Committee for Industrial Organization (CIO) in 1935. Lewis began working in the coal mines when he was twelve years old in 1892. He organized the coal industry and led its workers in several nationwide strikes. He died on June 11, 1970.

COAL STRIKE OF 1946 — led by John L. Lewis, then president of the United Mine Workers. Under his leadership, 400,000 coal miners went on strike for better pay and working conditions as well as a more substantial pension fund. Secretary of the Interior Julius A. Krug served as the main negotiator in drafting a contract acceptable to the mine workers. However, Mr. Lewis rejected the contract because he found a certain clause concerning vacation pay unsatisfactory. The United States Government, under President Truman's orders, sought an injunction which forbade the mining union to break the contract. Supported by the courts, the government fined the United Mine Workers and John L. Lewis $3,510,000 for civil and criminal contempt of court. The enormous amount of the penalty forced the striking workers to resume their jobs in the mines.

RAILROAD STRIKE OF 1946 — forced President Truman to take drastic measures because the railroads were almost solely responsible for transporting food and fuel across America. He called a joint session of Congress in hopes of enacting legislation which would allow him to draft strikers into the armed forces regardless of age or other considerations. The legislation's purpose was to break a strike which kept the nation from functioning properly. However, at the moment when Truman was about to present his proposal to Congress, he received a message from the railroad union officials informing him that they had consented to end the strike. The announcement was met with much cheering and applause in Congress.

SEIZURE OF STEEL MILLS — authorized by President Truman. When steel mill workers went on strike in 1946, the government seized the mills. This swift action ended the strike. However, when the steel workers went on strike again in 1952, the Supreme Court of the United States ruled it illegal for a President to order the seizure of a major industry. Therefore, the steel workers won the higher wages and better hours which they had been seeking.

TAFT-HARTLEY ACT — also known as the Labor Management Act of 1947. It formed a National Labor Management Panel to advise labor unions and management in order to help them solve their differences, especially those affecting the overall welfare of the United States.

A BOLD PLAN OF ACTION

As Truman had predicted, the Russians soon began to threaten the independence of other nations. In 1946, the Soviets tried to muscle their way into Iran and Turkey and they encouraged a Communist takeover of Greece. Since Greece and Turkey were important pathways in the shipment of oil from Iran to Great Britain, the freedom of those countries was vital.

To combat the Communists, both Greece and Turkey needed more military support than the British were able to provide. With the approval of Congress, Truman sent needed food and medical supplies to those countries and ordered U.S. ships into the Eastern Mediterranean to warn the Russians to move back. The maneuver worked. America's firm action forced the Russians to withdraw from Iran. It helped Turkey maintain control of the Bosporus and Dardanelles. In Greece, the anti-Communist forces won the civil war.

By making this bold move, Truman gave notice to the Russians that the United States planned to actively resist Communist aggression. This approach to combating foreign intervention in free countries is known as the Truman Doctrine.

Truman stressed that his foreign policy objectives were:

. . . to make the whole world a fair and good place where people can live, . . . to do away with revolutions and civil wars that kill people because a few factions can't agree with each other.

I was anxious that the humblest man in the farthest corner of the earth could have enough to eat, a place to sleep and ample clothes to wear. And I was willing to expend every effort . . . to get that done.

TRUMAN DOCTRINE — designed to contain Soviet Communist aggression. Becoming effective on March 12, 1947, it stated that the United States must "help free peoples to maintain their free institutions and their national integrity." The Truman Doctrine was first applied to the 1947 Communist infiltration of Turkey and Greece and was further tested during the Berlin Airlift. This doctrine has served as a guide to United States military participation in countries threatened by Communism.

THE TRUMAN-MARSHALL PLAN

During the next three years, Truman was instrumental in the development of one of the most farsighted and successful foreign policies ever made by the United States. It became known as the Marshall Plan. Since Truman had outlined the original idea, some people might argue that, in reality, it should have been called the *Truman Plan* for the Reconstruction of Europe.

Because Truman had witnessed the devastation and widespread starvation which resulted from World War I, he didn't want such a tragedy repeated following World War II. He believed that the prosperous nations had a moral responsibility to help feed the people of defeated nations until they could take care of themselves. He was also firmly convinced that if we helped those nations rebuild their peacetime industries and establish a strong economy, they would soon become welcome allies to the free world.

With Secretary of State George C. Marshall, President Truman molded the plan and presented it to Congress and to the other prosperous nations. The plan was quickly accepted and George C. Marshall was appointed coordinator of the program. Instead of forcing European nations to struggle by themselves, under the Marshall Plan over thirteen billion dollars were poured into those war-torn countries. It was a bold and ingenious plan — and it worked.

Major reconstruction efforts began within a month in Europe's cities. The agricultural production of Europe dramatically increased. As Europeans ate better and felt more secure, their industrial production leaped forward and soon exceeded prewar levels. In addition, trade between the United States and Europe boomed.

"It was the first time in the history of the world," Truman said later with justifiable pride, "that the victor has helped restore the vanquished to a normal way of life."

With George C. Marshall.

GEORGE C. MARSHALL — Chief of Staff of the Armed Forces from 1939 to 1945. During World War II, he was President Franklin D. Roosevelt's foremost strategic warfare adviser and was responsible for the overall organization and direction of American troops. All United States Army leaders, including Generals Eisenhower and MacArthur, were under his direct supervision. When the war ended in 1945, Marshall was appointed General of the Army, a newly created rank. In addition, he actively participated in the reconstruction of a war-torn Europe and Far East through the Marshall Plan. He served from 1945 to 1947 as President Truman's ambassador to China and later as his Secretary of Defense until retiring in 1951. He died in 1959 at the age of seventy-nine.

MARSHALL PLAN — composed to aid in the distribution of economic aid to a war-torn Europe and Far East. The objective of the Marshall Plan was to make these regions of the world self-supporting again by 1951. It required countries desiring economic aid to draw up an estimate concerning the amount of money needed for the reconstruction of their factories, railroads, farms, and transportation systems. Money, supplies, and machinery were then provided according to the precise amount assessed by each nation.

THE ESTABLISHMENT OF ISRAEL

During World War II, there were many reports that the Nazis were arresting thousands of European Jews and placing them in concentration camps. Rumors spread that the Third Reich had begun torturing and killing these people by the thousands. When Germany surrendered, the world learned that reality was worse than the rumors — the numbers of those persons who were tortured and killed were not totaled in thousands but in millions.

Between 1939 and 1945, over ten million European Jews were held captive in the cruelest conditions. Of those imprisoned, the Nazis killed over six million men, women, and children. In sheer numbers alone, the incarceration and wholesale murder of these European Jews compose the most heinous crimes ever devised and executed in the history of the world.

Despite objections from the Allies and even some Americans, President Truman insisted that those Germans accused of war crimes must not be executed without proper trials. He also wanted the people of the world to realize the extent of the crimes perpetrated by the Nazis.

Because he didn't want anyone ever to suggest that the charges against these men were unwarranted, Truman urged for all evidence be made public. Since the Germans kept detailed records and even took photographs and made motion pictures documenting the suffering they inflicted upon millions of people, the volume of evidence was staggering. Due to Truman's determination, the trials were scheduled and many German criminals of World War II were finally prosecuted, setting a precedent for future generations.

The four million surviving Jews were left homeless. Many did not want to return to the countries where they had previously lived. Instead, they wanted to establish a nation of their own in Palestine. The British, who controlled Palestine at the time, were against the idea. They knew that the Palestinian people would violently oppose Jewish occupation of the land.

President Truman was deeply moved by the horrors the Jewish people had suffered at the hands of the Nazis. Due to his familiarity with Bible history and his Baptist upbringing, Truman believed that the Jews had rights to at least a section of their ancestral land which is also the geographic center of their religion. He urged Great Britain to allow the Jews to establish the state of Israel. When the British hesitated, he threatened to cut back sorely needed economic aid to Great Britain.

Finally, the British gave in and on May 14, 1948, Israel became an independent state. The following day, Jewish leaders declared the existence of the state of Israel. At President Truman's urgent request, the United States of America was the first nation to recognize the Israeli government.

NAZI — follower of Adolf Hitler. While strongly favoring German territorial expansion and superiority, the Nazis demonstrated against Jewish people and democracy.

NUREMBURG TRIALS — held from 1945 to 1949 in the old city of Nuremburg, located ninety-two miles northwest of Munich, Germany. These trials involved the prosecution of twenty-two top-ranking leaders of Hitler's Third Reich. The accused were charged with having committed war crimes which included such deeds as prompting the outbreak of war as well as the murder and enslavement of Allied soldiers and innocent civilians. In addition, some of the defendants participated in the horrendous annihilation of millions of Jews and political prisoners in German concentration camps. Seven of the twenty-two men accused were found guilty on every charge and died by hanging. Three men were acquitted and seven given life imprisonments. Herman Goering, Hitler's chosen successor, committed suicide. In the American zone, twelve additional trials took place in relation to war crimes performed by German military leaders, chief officials in the SS (Hitler's secret police), industrialists, government officials, and Nazi judges as well as doctors who had committed heinous experiments on concentration camp prisoners. Many of the criminals were executed; some were given pardons or long-term prison sentences.

DAVID BEN-GURION — Israel's first Prime Minister. As a young man, he began a movement in 1919 toward the creation of a Jewish homeland in Palestine. His goal was finally achieved when Israel became a nation in 1948. He served as its Prime Minister until 1953 and again between 1955 and 1963. Born in Plonsk, Russia, Mr. Ben-Gurion died in Israel on December 1, 1973, at eighty-seven years of age.

THE BIG LIFT

As Russia tightened its control over the Eastern European nations it occupied, a ragged line of contention was being drawn through Europe. That line divided the democratic free countries of Western Europe from the Communist controlled nations in the east. During a visit to the United States, Winston Churchill gave that dividing line a name. In a speech to the faculty and students at Missouri's Westminster College on March 3, 1946, Churchill proclaimed:

*A shadow has fallen upon the scene so lately lighted by the Allied victory. Nobody knows what Soviet Russia and its Communist international organization intends to do . . . From Stettin in the Baltic to Trieste in the Adriatic, an **iron curtain** has descended across the Continent.*

Immediately following the speech, newspapers printed the term **"iron curtain"** in bold headlines. The iron curtain had not been drawn in the heat of battle, but during a nonmilitary "cold war" which existed between the anti-Communist and Communist nations.

At the close of World War II, the defeated Germany was divided into four military zones, each separately occupied by American, British, French, and Russian troops. The former capital city of Berlin was divided in the same manner, although it was one hundred and ten miles inside the Russian zone. Such a division had been agreed upon by Roosevelt at the Yalta Conference.

Because of the Marshall Plan's enormous success, the "cold war" was about to grow hot. In a move to force the United States, Great Britain, and France to abandon their sectors of Berlin, on June 24, 1948, the Russians blockaded all roads, canals, and railways along the East German border.

But Truman refused to desert West Berlin. He announced to the members of his cabinet, "We are going to stay. Period!"

Truman acted swiftly. On June 26, 1948, he ordered all U.S. Air Force cargo planes in Europe to begin flying supplies into the city. In a period of sixteen months, American and British airplanes made more than 250,000 flights and delivered more than two million tons of food and necessary supplies to West Berlin. Aviation experts consider the airlift a marvel of technology and organization.

The Berlin Airlift convinced the West Germans that they should ally their country with the nations of the free world. It also proved to Russia that the United States kept its commitments. Finally realizing the failure of their plan, the Russians called off the blockade.

And international respect grew even stronger for the determination and genius of the President of the United States—Harry S. Truman.

Winston Churchill admitted that when Truman first took office, he was concerned that this man from Missouri might lack the abilities of forceful leadership. "I misjudged you badly," he later told Truman. "Since that time, you more than any other man have saved Western Civilization."

COLD WAR — a conflict where no actual fighting occurs. The term was first coined by Bernard Baruch, an American statesman. In a cold war, the ideologies of communism and democracy continuously grate at each other. This conflict is constantly being kindled by economic and political weapons as well as propaganda. However, the danger of a "hot war" is ever present. This more familiar kind of war would involve powerful military armaments, the shedding of human blood, and the possible downfall of entire governments and nations.

UNIFYING THE AMERICAS

With Russia threatening aggression in Europe and Asia, President Truman realized the importance of building stronger relationships with the nations of the Western Hemisphere. In 1947, he personally visited Canada, Mexico, and Brazil.

It was the first state visit undertaken by a President of the United States to Mexico and he was greeted by cheering crowds.

In Canada, Truman spoke to a joint session of the Parliament and stressed the determination of the United States to deter Communist aggression wherever it occurred. He received a standing ovation.

In the summer of 1947, representatives from twenty American nations met in Brazil for the International Conference for the Maintenance of Continental Peace and Security. During the meetings, the members agreed to sign a pact which forbade any one country to attack another nation in our hemisphere. If one tried, the others promised to join forces to rebuff the aggressor.

The conference was a diplomatic triumph for the United States. President Truman was so pleased by the results that he decided to travel to Brazil and personally sign the agreement. The Brazilians and the delegates were delighted. They enthusiastically welcomed the President and his family.

As Truman was being heralded throughout the world as a great leader who possessed astute insight and bold ideas, the people of the United States only thought of him as the man who was completing Roosevelt's term of office. Many newspapers were highly critical of Truman's trips to foreign countries and expressed the attitude, "Who does this little man from Missouri think he is?"

Although the citizens of the United States questioned Truman's stature, there was certainly no doubt in the minds of the people of other nations. They knew who he was — he was the President of the United States.

THE WALKING PRESIDENT

Harry Truman's habitual early morning walks became so widely known that he was often referred to as the "Walking President."

Whether in Washington, D.C., or visiting another city, he was up early and, flanked by secret service men, Truman would set out on a morning walk. His pace was so brisk that he often left news reporters and cameramen several steps behind gasping for breath.

During his walks, his disregard for personal safety kept the secret service men constantly alert. Perhaps the most refreshing quality Truman exhibited as President was his eagerness to visit with people he met.

When people gathered on the sidewalks, Truman delighted in greeting them, shaking their hands and engaging in friendly conversations. When seeing someone hesitate to approach him, he often walked straight to the person and introduced himself.

There was little doubt that Truman liked people and he enjoyed talking with shopkeepers, farmers, and day laborers. He shared a common bond with average citizens and they readily felt he understood and cared about their problems.

While many people who saw him during his morning walks would say, "Good morning, Mr. President," there were often many who would simply call out, "Hi, Harry!" He saw no disrespect in such greetings. In fact, he seemed to enjoy knowing they felt moved to greet him by his first name.

THE WHITE HOUSE BLUES

Not long after the Trumans moved into the White House, they began to notice that the floors were extremely unsteady. The President called the Commissioner of Public Buildings and asked him to survey the structure. Several weeks later the engineers reported that the second floor was dangerously close to collapsing — "the only thing holding it up was habit."

Architects and engineers began bracing floors. The first floor and the Truman living quarters were interrupted by a maze of beams and steel braces. The work wasn't started soon enough, however, for the old building began to fall apart in the summer of 1948. One Sunday afternoon a spinet piano in Margaret's sitting room broke through the floor. Fortunately, the piano did not fall completely through the ceiling. If it had, it would have landed in the dining room directly below.

When the Truman family returned from a trip to Missouri on November 7, 1948, the architects and engineers refused to allow them to enter because the building wasn't safe. While the inside of the White House was completely gutted and rebuilt with proper steel bracing, the Trumans moved into the Blair House where they resided for the next three years.

WHITE HOUSE — the official home of American Presidents. Originally designed by James Hoban, its construction began in 1792. President John Adams occupied the residence in 1800 when construction was nearly complete. From 1809 to 1817, President Thomas Jefferson directed the final stages of the building; however, the War of 1812 left the White House partially burned and extensive remodeling was required. Benjamin H. Latrobe, an architect, lent his talents and services to the reconstruction of the executive mansion. Renovation of the White House during the Truman Administration cost $5,700,000.

BLAIR HOUSE — located directly across from the White House on Pennsylvania Avenue in Washington, D.C. In 1824, Dr. Joseph Lovell, the first surgeon general of the United States Army, constructed the four-story yellow stucco home. The house was bought in 1836 by Francis Preston Blair, Sr., who happened to be a member of President Andrew Jackson's Cabinet. Purchased by the United States Government from the Blair family in 1942, it has since housed presidential guests.

A HOUSE IS NOT A HOME

During the reconstruction of the White House, the number of rooms increased from sixty-two to one hundred and seven. The third floor was made into a full story and the basement was expanded. The inside was totally redecorated but Truman insisted that the historic rooms, which were familiar to the public, be carefully restored to their original design.

It seemed that little could happen in the world without someone trying to blame Harry Truman. Completely disregarding the fact that the White House was ready to collapse, there were those who criticized the President for urging Congress to appropriate the money to have it reconstructed. When it was fully realized how very close the nation had come to losing a historic monument, the snide remarks finally subsided.

The Trumans took their move to the Blair House in stride. In fact, Mrs. Truman and Margaret enjoyed the comfort and furnishings of Blair House more than those in the White House.

News reporters discovered that Mrs. Truman was a very strong-willed woman who preferred her privacy. She steadfastly refused to make public comments about political issues or people. She firmly believed that maintaining a stable home environment for her husband and daughter was her first duty. Although she attended official functions and social events, she gave the reporters very little to write about.

Mrs. Truman's personality and personal views have remained somewhat private. Through the years, the news media and the American people began to sense that she was a person of strong character who neither required or wanted attention and couldn't be swayed by flattery. They also became aware that she had a keen sense of humor.

During the time that Mrs. Truman was First Lady, dinners and social events at the White House or at Blair House may not have been as elaborate as those of other administrations, but they were always carefully prepared and beautifully planned. The nation's reporters and the American people grew to respect her immensely and developed a fond regard for her. That seemed to be the way she wanted it.

With Mrs. Truman and Margaret.

THE CHINA DISCONNECTION

During his first term as President, no problem was more troublesome to Truman than that of China. While the maps of the 1940s showed China as one gigantic country, it was really divided by three opposing forces. The Russian Communists occupied Manchuria. The Chinese Communists, led by Mao Tse-tung, controlled the North. The Nationalist forces of General Chiang Kai-shek governed the South.

Before the Japanese invasion in 1939, China was already embroiled in a civil war. But in order to repel the Japanese, the Communist and Nationalist forces called a temporary truce.

During the war, Americans heard more about Chiang Kai-shek's Nationalist Army than they did about the Communists. Chiang's wife made several trips to the United States to thank the American people for their support in combating the Japanese. The newspaper reporters and newsreel cameras gave her visits widespread publicity. To the American people, Chiang Kai-shek was the undisputed leader of China. This was far from the truth.

As soon as the war with Japan ended, the Nationalists and the Communists resumed battling each other for control of China. In an attempt to stop the bloodshed, Truman sent General George C. Marshall to mediate a cease-fire between the two opposing forces. On January 13, 1946, Chiang and Mao signed an agreement but the armistice was not long lasting. Within a few short months fighting broke out once more.

Since political and public opinion in this country was on the side of the Nationalists, the United States sent over two billion dollars worth of aid to Chiang's forces. However, some of Chiang's generals were corrupt and sold much of the military equipment and supplies to the other side. Due to the disorganization of the Nationalist armies, the Communist forces swept through the southern provinces and forced the Nationalist army and their followers to flee from the mainland and settle on the island of Formosa (Taiwan).

CHIANG KAI-SHEK — founder of Nationalist China. Born in 1887, he became a general in the Chinese Army and, later, a statesman. He governed China from 1926 until 1949 when the Communist forces of Mao Tse-tung ousted him from power. Chiang fled with his followers to the island of Taiwan, formerly known as Formosa. There he ruled until he died on April 5, 1975.

MAO TSE-TUNG — founder of the People's Republic of China. With the support of his revolutionary Communist forces, he drove Chiang Kai-shek from power in September of 1949. Mao remained active as chairman of the Chinese Communist Party until his death on September 9, 1976, at the age of eighty-three.

THE BUCK STOPS — ALMOST

The news media and many Americans unjustly blamed President Truman for "losing China." In truth, it was the corruption and disintegration within the Nationalist Party which lost China. The only way Truman could have "saved" China would have been to send in United States troops. Having just experienced the largest war ever waged, neither Truman nor the American people were ready to become involved in another.

By now, President Truman was growing used to shouldering unjust accusations. On his desk in the Oval Office, he had placed a small wooden plaque which read, "The Buck Stops Here." He was ready and able to make necessary decisions and he had the courage to withstand unfavorable public opinion.

No one expected or wanted Harry S. Truman to run for another term of office. Some leaders of the Democratic Party openly urged President Truman to step down and offer his support to another candidate. The American people didn't expect him to run. They felt that Harry Truman had completed Roosevelt's term of office and now he should allow the people to choose a "real" President.

Believing he had no chance of winning the election, his close friends advised him to retire. Even members of his own family, who felt his splendid efforts as President had not been offered proper respect, wanted him to return to private life.

THE BUCK STOPS HERE — the place or person who is given or accepts final responsibility. The phrase derives from "pass the buck" which means to transfer the responsibility or blame to another place or person.

NO WAY TO WIN

The political atmosphere and the sequence of events of the 1948 presidential election were both confusing and surprising. They also formed one of the most fascinating stories in the history of American politics and the biggest electoral upset of the century.

Harry Truman was simply not going to allow the Democratic Party and the American people to drop him by the wayside. He believed he had taken too much unfair criticism from newspapers, political leaders, and labor unions. He was determined to let the people hear his side before he left office. He didn't want to go down in history as the man who finished Roosevelt's term of office. He wanted to be elected to the Presidency in his own right.

Ironically, the economy of the country had never been better. The American people ate better, made more money, lived in larger houses, drove bigger cars, read more books, wore more expensive clothes, and took more vacations than at any other period in known history. In such circumstances, the incumbent President would normally be assured of reelection. But not in Truman's case.

He had several other strikes against him. The Democratic Party was in an upheaval. The news media was strongly Republican. The number of labor strikes and the Chinese revolution had lowered the nation's opinion of their President. And there was strong public opinion that after sixteen years of leadership, the Democrats had controlled the presidential office long enough. It was time for a change. All agreed that there was no possible way he could win the election. Every one seemed to agree except one man — Harry S. Truman.

TRUMAN'S SURPRISE DECISION

In March of 1948, the chairman of the Democratic National Committee, J. Howard McGrath, gave a surprising announcement to the press — Truman had decided to run for reelection. In May, President Truman spoke to a gathering of Young Democrats.

"I tell you," he stated boldly, "for the next four years, there will be a Democrat in the White House — and you're looking at him!"

Although they could hardly believe he actually thought he might win, those present applauded; if not because of their enthusiasm, then surely with respect for Harry Truman's nerve to challenge such enormous odds.

In a state of shock and some newfound admiration, the news reporters wrote their headlines proclaiming:

"TRUMAN DECIDES TO RUN FOR RE-ELECTION!"

When people read Truman's announcement in the morning papers, those who didn't laugh shook their heads in disbelief. The Republicans were delighted with Truman's decision. They were now convinced that no matter who they nominated, that person would win. At the Republican Convention in June, they selected their candidate — Thomas E. Dewey of New York. Dewey had an impressive record in public life. He was a polished speaker and, having run against Franklin Roosevelt four years before, he was already nationally known.

The Republicans felt victory in their grasp.

The Democrats were ready to accept defeat.

It was all but concluded that Thomas E. Dewey would be the next President of the United States and Truman would go home to Independence, Missouri.

But Harry Truman wasn't ready to go home — not yet!

THOMAS DEWEY — campaigned twice on the Republican ticket for the Presidency and was defeated by Franklin D. Roosevelt in 1944 and Harry S. Truman in 1948. Born on March 24, 1902, in Owosso, Michigan, he studied law at Columbia University, and in 1933 he began serving as the United States attorney for New York State's southern district. In 1935, he was selected by Governor Herman Lehman to be a special prosecutor in vice and racket investigations. He acted as Governor of New York from 1943 to 1955 and then resumed his law practice. Mr. Dewey died in 1971.

THE WHISTLE-STOP CAMPAIGN

Although Harry Truman fully realized his campaign would be an uphill battle, he was determined to give it everything he had. Perhaps those persons who repeatedly predicted he didn't have a chance were not aware (or had forgotten or never knew) how a younger Truman had campaigned for judge in Jackson County and had run for the Missouri Senate. He had won those elections by going straight to the people, city by city and town by town. But those had been local and regional elections. Could such a campaign be conducted on a national scale from coast to coast? No one knew — not even Truman — but he intended to find out.

When the University of California invited the President to deliver the commencement address, Truman immediately accepted the invitation. On June 3, 1948, he boarded a special train and began a journey which would take him all the way from Washington, D.C., to the West Coast and back. Since he was not yet his party's candidate, Truman could not officially campaign for office. But Truman had the train stop in dozens of cities along the way. From the observation platform he spoke to people who came to the stations to see him.

Since he had never been comfortable reading prepared speeches, he discarded them. He began to speak directly to his audience with a zestful, off-the-cuff approach. In his speeches he explained his positions on issues of the day, criticized "that do nothing Eightieth Congress," and answered questions frankly and honestly. The approach worked. The crowds loved it!

In Albuquerque, New Mexico, an incident happened which gave the Truman campaign an enduring label.

In the middle of one of his fiery speeches a listener suddenly shouted out, "Lay it on, Harry! Give 'em hell!"

Truman immediately replied, "I intend to."

And the audience cheered for this "scrappy little fighter."

The trip was an enormous success and the "Give 'em hell" campaign was on its way.

It was evident to everyone who attended the Democratic Convention in July, 1948, that Harry Truman was determined to be the Democratic candidate. Due to the lack of unity and leadership in the party, there was no way anyone could stop him.

While the atmosphere of the Republican Convention, which had been held a month earlier, was jubilant, the Democratic Convention was one of gloom. During one of the keynote speeches Senator Alben Barkley, the Senate minority leader, momentarily brought the proceedings to life by offering a rousingly sentimental speech. It caused such a stir that the convention selected him to be the candidate for Vice-President. Although Truman would much rather have picked someone else, he was given no choice. So, he graciously accepted Barkley as his running mate.

Two days later, Senator Hubert H. Humphrey of Minnesota energetically led a successful movement to get Truman's civil rights program written into the Democratic Platform. The delegates from the Southern states, led by Governor Strom Thurmond of South Carolina, were so outraged that they pulled out of the Democratic Party. When a reporter mentioned to Thurmond that President Truman was only following the civil rights platform previously set by Roosevelt, Thurmond answered, "I agree. But Truman means it."

The Southern group decided to form a third party of their own, the "Dixiecrats," and ran Thurmond for the Presidency. The newspapers and the pollsters were now completely convinced that the Republicans would move Thomas E. Dewey into the White House.

Nevertheless, Truman still wasn't ready to admit defeat. Instead, he hit the campaign trail with increased vigor. Joined by Bess and Margaret, he boarded the train called the "Truman Special" and started another cross-country tour.

ALBEN BARKLEY — Vice-President of the United States under President Truman from 1949 to 1953. Born in 1877 at Graves County, Kentucky, he served seven consecutive terms in the House of Representatives beginning in 1913 and was Kentucky's Senator from 1927 to 1949. During his Vice-Presidency, he exercised great skill in presiding over the Senate. He was the first Vice-President to sit on the National Security Council which creates important policies for the President's consideration. When his term as Vice-President ended, he resumed his senatorial duties until his death in 1956.

THE CROWDS GROW LARGER

The distance he traveled and the number of speeches he gave were astounding. From June to November of 1948, Truman made seven major trips in which he logged almost thirty-two thousand miles. On those trips, he made over 355 speeches, sometimes as many as sixteen a day. Such a schedule would have worn down most men but, as one writer observed, "When the going was toughest, he could make a speech at one whistle-stop and then sleep...and make another thirty minutes later....Strain seemed only to make him calmer and firmer."

Although they began to admire Truman's nerve, the Republicans, the pollsters, and the newsmen staunchly maintained that all of his energies were being expended for nothing. Even when they saw that the crowds greeting Truman at railroad stations were growing larger and larger, they quickly concluded that those people were only curious to see what the outgoing President looked like. As Truman's speeches began to receive more and more applause, it was concluded that the audiences were merely being polite; they would never express the same courtesy in votes.

The people, however, were becoming acquainted with Harry Truman and his family and grew to like their straightforward manners. Most important, they listened to what Truman said. He spoke so simply and with such conviction that the audiences began to believe him.

Four days before the election the polls still showed Dewey to be far ahead of Truman. But Truman maintained he didn't believe in polls. He insisted he "believed in the American people." Again, he firmly predicted that, despite what everyone else said, Harry S. Truman would win the election.

THE UPSET OF THE CENTURY

On election morning, Harry Truman, Bess, and Margaret voted. After attending a luncheon in Independence, Missouri, the President, accompanied by three secret service men, quietly left the building unnoticed by the reporters and drove thirty miles to Excelsior Springs. They checked into the Elms Hotel. Away from prying reporters and gathering crowds, the President relaxed, enjoyed a Turkish bath, ate a ham sandwich, listened to the early election returns, and went to bed.

At about midnight, President Truman awoke and listened to the radio reports for a few minutes. He heard he was ahead of Dewey by over one million votes. When the announcer said Truman was still predicted to lose, the President turned over and went back to sleep.

At 4:00 a.m. he was awakened by one of his secret service men. He learned that he was two million votes ahead. One of the leading radio commentators, however, still maintained that, when all the votes were counted, Dewey would win hands down. Truman laughed, told the secret service man not to awaken him again, and went back to sleep.

The following morning those same newsmen were stunned by the final results. The impossible had happened. That "scrappy little fighter" from Independence, Missouri, had proved them all wrong. Harry S. Truman had won the election.

On his way back to Washington, D.C., aboard the "Truman Special," someone handed the newly elected President the early morning edition of the *Chicago Daily Tribune*. Harry Truman read the headline, laughed heartily, and held it up for a cheering crowd to see. Believing the predictions, the newspaper editors had jumped the gun. To their own embarrassment, the main headline purported:

DEWEY DEFEATS TRUMAN.

On January 20, 1949, Harry S. Truman repeated the oath of office for a second time. He was the President of the United States of America, no longer completing another man's term of office but beginning his own. By his determination and persistence, Harry Truman had created the greatest political upset of the century.

"...BUT TRUMAN MEANS IT!"

Critics claim that Harry Truman wasn't interested in supporting civil rights until the black vote helped him win the 1948 election. Those who make such charges either don't know what they are talking about or have chosen to ignore Truman's earlier efforts.

As early as 1940, long before anyone thought of him as a possible President, Harry Truman spoke to a group of black people at the Democratic Convention in Chicago. In his speech, which was later reprinted in the *Congressional Record*, he frankly said:

> We all know that the Negro is here to stay and in no way can be removed from our political and economic life, and we should recognize his inalienable rights as specified in our Constitution. Can any man claim protection of our laws if he denies that protection to others?

Again, in 1940, while speaking at Sedalia, Missouri, to open his bid for reelection to the Missouri Senate, he said:

> I believe in the brotherhood of man, not merely the brotherhood of white men but the brotherhood of all men before law.
>
> I believe in the Constitution and the Declaration of Independence. In giving the Negroes the rights which are theirs, we are only acting in accord with our own ideals of a true democracy.
>
> If any class or race can be permanently set apart from, or pushed down below, the rest in political and civil rights, so may any other class or race when it shall incur the displeasure of its more powerful associates, and we may say farewell to the principles on which we count our safety.

As President, Truman displayed his determination to improve black civil rights. On December 5, 1946, he appointed a Committee on Civil Rights and in January of 1947 he instructed its members:

> I want our Bill of Rights implemented in fact. We have been trying to do this for 150 years. We're making progress, but we're not making progress fast enough.

When the committee released its report four months later, its findings made national headlines. The committee did more than cite the nation's ailments in civil rights; it also laid out a program to cure those ills.

On February 2, 1948, Harry Truman made one of the most daring civil rights speeches and took one of the biggest political gambles of any President in history. In a special message to Congress, he stressed:

> *We shall not . . . finally achieve the ideals for which this nation was founded so long as any American suffers discrimination as a result of his race, or religion, or color, or the land of origin of his forefathers.*
>
> *We cannot be satisfied until all our people have equal opportunity for jobs, for homes, for education, for health and for political expression, and until all our people have equal protection under the law.*

He asked Congress to back a program to secure civil rights for all American citizens which would include the following ten points:

1. A permanent commission on civil rights, a joint Congressional committee on civil rights, and a civil rights division of the Department of Justice.
2. The strengthening of existing civil rights statutes.
3. Federal protection against lynching.
4. More adequate protection of the right to vote.
5. A federal Fair Employment Practices Commission.
6. A ban on discrimination in interstate transportation.
7. Home rule for the District of Columbia.
8. Statehood for Hawaii and Alaska and more self-government for other U.S. territories.
9. Equalizing opportunities for residents of the United States to become naturalized citizens.
10. Settlement of the evacuation claims of Japanese-Americans.

DESEGREGATES ARMED SERVICES

Truman became the first President to unequivocally say that the federal government has the responsibility to secure civil rights for people of minority groups.

Even though his proposals received hostile reaction from Southern congressmen, and some even made threats to sabotage the Marshall Plan if the President didn't curb his views, Truman refused to back down.

Outraged by the unjust treatment and segregation of black servicemen and women in the Armed Forces and the unfair employment practices in governmental jobs, Harry Truman, as President and Commander in Chief of the Armed Forces, issued an executive order on July 26, 1948, barring segregation in the Armed Forces and prohibiting discrimination in federal employment.

While addressing a commencement audience at Howard University in 1952, Harry Truman stressed, "You can't cure a moral problem or a social problem by ignoring it."

In later years, some critics have proposed that Truman should have done more in the field of civil rights. But if they consider the climate of the time in which he was President, they may be amazed that he had the courage and the fortitude to accomplish so much.

THE NATO ALLIANCE

When the American voters reelected Harry S. Truman as President, it is doubtful that many realized they were really electing an international leader. His insights and abilities for placing new concepts into action were destined to alter the course of the world.

With the success of the Marshall Plan and the Truman Doctrine, President Truman and Secretary of State Dean Acheson began considering another problem — the conditions in the underdeveloped countries throughout the world. As Great Britain, France, and other larger industrial nations began granting independence to the countries they had colonized, it became obvious to President Truman that in order for those countries to remain independent and prosper, they needed assistance in developing their natural and industrial resources.

As Point Four of his Four-Point Program for maintaining peace in the world, President Truman proposed that the United States "must embark on a bold new program for making the benefits of our scientific advances and industrial progress available for the improvement of underdeveloped areas." He insisted that the United States help other nations help themselves because the peace of the world was dependent upon the well-being, self-government, and freedom of all nations. He saw this course as the political and moral obligation of the United States to the future of the world. The goal of improving the living conditions and the governments of other countries is perhaps the most unselfish approach ever undertaken by a powerful nation in the history of the world.

To discourage and resist Russia's desire to dominate Western Europe and the Middle East, Truman urged the formation of the North Atlantic Treaty Organization (NATO). Twelve nations agreed to come to the aid of any one of the nations should it fall subject to attack. The formal alliance was signed in Washington, D.C., on April 4, 1949. Although many in this country criticized the formation of NATO, Truman held fast to his belief that the safety of the United States was interrelated with the freedom of Western Europe.

In 1947, after a considerable struggle, Truman managed to unify the Armed Forces by placing them under what would become the Department of Defense. The National Security Act of 1947 also provided for the formation of the Central Intelligence Agency (CIA) to gather and distribute information in regard to national defense and security.

NATO — the North Atlantic Treaty Organization. In 1949, the United States, Canada, Great Britain, France, Belgium, Norway, the Netherlands, Iceland, Italy, Denmark, Portugal, Luxembourg, and Greece as well as Turkey joined in this alliance to develop a unified front against Communist advancement in Europe.

THE GREAT AMERICAN TRAGEDY

As the Cold War with Russia grew even more hostile in Western Europe, it was learned that for some time a network of spies had been passing information concerning atomic research and development to the Russians.

In 1948, Whittaker Chambers, a senior editor of *Time Magazine,* confessed to having been a former Communist and charged that Alger Hiss, a man who had held several high governmental positions, had given secret documents to the Russians. Although Hiss denied the charges, he was placed on trial in 1950. Hiss was found guilty of perjury and sentenced to prison.

The incident triggered a rash of charges and countercharges of Communist infiltration, not only in government offices but in defense industries, the entertainment world and news media, and the field of education as well. Allegations and suspicions mushroomed into a nationwide fear of a Communist takeover.

Sensing the widespread terror, Senator Joseph McCarthy from Wisconsin grabbed the opportunity to gain national attention for himself. In a series of speeches, McCarthy stated that he had obtained the names of over 205 card-carrying Communists who were in the State Department. Claiming to have documents of unquestionable proof, McCarthy brashly made outlandish accusations and created an atmosphere of national hysteria.

A Senate subcommittee was appointed to investigate those charges. The hearings were televised and they captured the attention of millions of Americans.

Throughout the country, the American people sat before their television sets, listened to their radios, and read newspaper accounts of the hearings with stunned disbelief. They curiously watched and listened while McCarthy bullied those who testified. They saw careers destroyed and lifetimes of service shattered.

Even though President Truman had already established a Federal Commission on Employee Loyalty, McCarthy's vigilante attacks aimed toward the White House and charged that even President Truman was "soft on Communism." Although such accusations could not have been further from the truth, they forced the President into the uncomfortable position of defending himself and the White House staff. The rumors and attacks were slow in dying and they would plague the President throughout his last three years in office.

Denouncing McCarthy's charges, President Truman astutely assessed the situation. "It is one of the tragedies of our time," he said, "that the security program of the United States has been wickedly used by demagogues and sensational newspapers in an attempt to frighten and mislead the American people."

After months of continuous accusations and testimonies, it became obvious that McCarthy's information was a "colored and distorted version of material." And in time, historians would agree with Truman's assessment.

JOSEPH McCARTHY — born at Grand Chute, Wisconsin, in 1909. As a Republican Senator from 1946 to 1954, he presided over the House on Un-American Activities Committee between 1950 and 1954. The proceedings of this committee unjustly dealt with possible Communist infiltration into government, education, defense industries and other fields. During the time these hearings were being conducted, McCarthy wrote *America's Retreat from Victory* (1951) and *McCarthyism: The Fight for America* (1952). He died in 1957.

DOUGLAS MacARTHUR — born the son of a career soldier in Little Rock, Arkansas, in 1880. MacArthur graduated from West Point Military Academy in 1903, first in his class. During the Second World War, he became one of the most charismatic military generals in American history when serving as Supreme Commander of the Allied Forces in the Southwest Pacific. He returned to the Philippines in 1945, as promised, to liberate the Japanese occupied islands. In September of that same year, the Japanese surrendered to him on board the U.S.S. *Missouri*. Directly following the end of the war, he administered Japan's military and governmental affairs as well as the development of Japan into a democratic state. He won the respect of the Japanese people by his firm, but fair, policies. When relieved of his post in Japan, he was appointed Commander of U.S. Forces during a part of the 1951-1953 Korean conflict. He retired in 1951 and died thirteen years later in 1964.

THE KOREAN CRISIS

Although Russia's threats of aggression, the Communist takeover of China, and the hysteria of McCarthyism consumed the days and nights of the President — another international crisis was about to explode.

On Saturday evening, June 24, 1950, President Truman received a telephone call from Secretary of State Dean Acheson with urgent news: "The North Koreans have invaded South Korea!" Early the next morning, Truman instructed Acheson to meet with the service secretaries and chiefs of staffs to begin recommendations for action.

Although the South Korean Army was partially trained by United States military advisers, it was evident that it was a poor match for the invaders from the North. Truman immediately ordered United States forces to help the South Koreans. Fully aware that such tough action might trigger World War III, Truman was later to say that the decision of whether or not to send U.S. troops to assist South Korea was "most difficult" because he realized it "affected the whole free world." He knew that the Communists could not be allowed to take whatever territory they wanted.

In a historic resolution, the United States pledged its support. Within days, whole divisions of well-equipped United States and United Nations soldiers were sent into South Korea. It was one of the fastest buildups of armed forces the world has ever witnessed. General Douglas MacArthur, one of the great military leaders of World War II, was called away from overseeing the U.S. occupation of Japan to command the United States and United Nations forces in Korea.

By August, the Communist advance was successfully halted near the port of Pusan. On September 15, under MacArthur's command, the joint forces executed one of the most daring and successful military maneuvers in history. Large amphibious forces assaulted the west coast of Korea, and within forty-five days they had cut off the Communists' sources of supplies and had their army in full retreat. It appeared that the war was all but won.

THE PRESIDENT vs. THE GENERAL

Delighted with his victory, MacArthur was eager to take all of North Korea. Fearing that such action could ignite a war with China, President Truman decided to meet with the General face-to-face. A meeting was arranged for October 15 on Wake Island.

When Truman's plane arrived on Wake Island, General MacArthur was already there to greet the President.

Before reporters and cameramen, the President and the General flashed warm and friendly smiles. But beneath the display of cordiality, Truman was very annoyed. The General had worn his customary dark glasses and gold-braided hat. His shirt collar was casually unbuttoned as if he had stepped out for a morning stroll. Hardly fitting, Truman thought, for greeting the President of the United States and the Commander in Chief.

During the meeting, MacArthur assured Truman that the Korean conflict would be won before Christmas and that there was no reason to believe that China or Russia would give the North Koreans additional assistance. The meetings ended in a mood of optimism. On his way back home to the States, Truman hoped he and MacArthur had reached a workable understanding and that together they had offset a major confrontation with China and Russia.

But General MacArthur had other ideas.

As authorized by President Truman, MacArthur moved his forces beyond the 38th Parallel (which was the border established after World War II dividing North Korea from South Korea). But he was emphatically warned to proceed northward slowly so as not to unnecessarily alarm China.

Wanting another glorious victory on the record, MacArthur flagrantly disregarded the warning and encouraged his troops to surge north toward the Yalu River which separated North Korea from China's province of Manchuria. Not only did he act contrary to orders but he made a fatal error in judgment. On November 26, 1950, China unleashed an overwhelming attack, sending over 200,000 soldiers well equipped with tanks and artillery into North Korea. Taken by surprise, U.S. and U.N. divisions suffered heavy losses of men and weapons in a hasty and chaotic retreat.

When Truman learned that MacArthur had ignored orders, he could hardly believe the General's actions. Although in public the President controlled his anger, in private he was furious. "I didn't travel seven thousand miles for one of my generals to give me the wrong information," he fumed.

By March, the U.S. and U.N. forces had once more regrouped. They recaptured Seoul, the capital of South Korea, and finally pushed the invaders back to the 38th Parallel. The British and our European Allies felt the time was right to negotiate an armistice. Truman agreed and sent MacArthur a message informing him of the plan.

Before official negotiations could be started, however, General MacArthur undercut the diplomatic maneuver by issuing his own offer to negotiate a truce with the enemy "in the field" and, if his terms were not met, he threatened to attack China's mainland.

It was an extraordinary act of insubordination and another miscalculation on MacArthur's part. This time, he had indeed overestimated the importance of his popularity with the American people and his influence in Congress. He certainly underestimated Harry S. Truman. The President reacted decisively. He issued an order relieving the General of his command. Or, as Truman bluntly put it, "I fired him!"

When the news was released, a storm of public protest burst across the nation. Members of Congress and the press lashed out at Truman for publicly reprimanding a national hero. They insisted that MacArthur be reinstated. But Truman stood firm.

When MacArthur returned to the United States, more than seven and one-half million people lined the streets of New York City and gave him a hero's welcome. He was asked to speak to a joint session of Congress and, with the eloquence of a seasoned orator and the style of a polished actor, he dramatically ended his emotion-filled speech by quoting the line of a sentimental poem, "Old soldiers never die, they just fade away." He received a standing ovation.

General Matthew B. Ridgway replaced MacArthur as Commander of the U.N. forces in Korea. While a limited cease-fire was initiated in 1951, the war in Korea would not end for another two years. It was a long time before the American people and the news media were able to forgive Truman for firing MacArthur — and even longer before they realized he was right.

SUDDEN VIOLENCE

At about two o'clock on the afternoon of November 1, 1950, the serenity of Pennsylvania Avenue was shattered by a burst of gunfire. Two fanatic Puerto Rican nationalists, Oscar Collazo and Griselio Torresola, had walked up to the steps of Blair House. They pulled out guns and began firing at the policeman and secret service men who were stationed at the front door. In the next three minutes, thirty-two shots were exchanged. When it ended, one police officer had been wounded and another fatally shot. Collazo lay wounded at the foot of the front steps and his partner, Torresola, was dead.

Although there had been other assassination plots against President Truman, the two Puerto Ricans came dangerously close to their target. The President was only a few feet away, having just awakened from his usual afternoon nap in the upstairs bedroom.

When the excitement was over, the President calmly left Blair House on schedule for a speaking engagement. At the dedication of a statue of Field Marshall Sir John Dill at Arlington Cemetery, President Truman said of the assassination attempt, "A President has to expect these things."

The attackers' choice of Truman as a target is ironic because he had championed the cause of Puerto Rican independence.

Although in the following days secret service men tried to persuade him to take stricter precautions, the President refused to stop his morning walks or to be seen less in public. Even though the incident greatly worried Mrs. Truman and Margaret, President Truman displayed no outward sign of concern.

A FAMILY UNITED

Despite the turmoil and the challenges of the office, Harry Truman enjoyed being the President of the United States. He functioned on the basis of, "If there's a job to do, do it." He had the ability to make important decisions and then move on to other matters without worrying.

There seemed to be a place for everything in his life and he tried to put everything in its place. Perhaps his Midwest upbringing provided him a strong basis for sorting the important from the unimportant and his early and continued interest in the military gave him a sense of order and regiment. When he was working he was all work. But when he had time to relax, he relaxed. There is little doubt that his family life was as solid as his professional one. He was a devoted husband to Bess and a doting father to Margaret.

BUT THE BOTTLE WOULDN'T BREAK

Mrs. Truman was a shy and private person. If the long hours and the demands on her as First Lady ever weighed too heavily, no one ever heard her complain. She accepted her roles as Harry S. Truman's wife and Margaret's mother as her first responsibilities and provided a warm and secure home. Somehow, she kept much of their family life apart from the arena of hectic political activities and world attention — an amazing feat.

When attending public functions, Mrs. Truman conducted herself with quiet dignity. In 1945, however, an incident occurred during one of her public appearances that would have unnerved even the most seasoned performer. Mrs. Truman had been asked to christen a new airplane. As newsreel cameras were rolling, she stepped forward onto the platform, took the bottle of champagne in her hands, and struck it against the nose of the craft. To her surprise, as well as that of the audience, the bottle didn't break.

The sequence of actions which followed compose one of the funniest newsreel films ever photographed. She hit the bottle against the plane again and again with no success — it just wouldn't break. On the last few tries, she was swinging it with the determination and stance of Joe DiMaggio, baseball's famed New York Yankee slugger.

Finally, an Air Force major gallantly took the bottle to finish the job for her. He slammed the bottle against the plane's nose with all his manly force — it still didn't break. But after several more attempts, the glass finally broke and champagne splashed over the nose of the plane and those standing on the platform. Although the incident must have been trying for Mrs. Truman and embarrassing to the Major, it's as funny to watch as a Laurel and Hardy comedy.

THE ANSWER IS NEVER!

President Truman appreciated and admired his wife's support. He respected her opinions and cherished her as his life's companion. He fully realized that being cast in the role of First Lady was an awesome responsibility. He had chosen his profession and, being a gregarious person, enjoyed the public attention. But he was aware that Mrs. Truman had not sought such a role. While he believed newsmen and political opponents had every right to criticize his actions, he was furious whenever anyone said or wrote unkind words about his wife.

In 1945, Henry Luce, one of the most prominent publishers in the United States (*Time*/*Life*) and husband of Clare Boothe Luce, a very successful playwright and editor, spoke to the President. After reminding Truman that he had made sizable contributions to the Democratic Party, Luce then asked why his wife, Clare, had never been invited to a White House function.

"Mr. Luce, you've asked a fair question and I'll give you a fair answer," President Truman replied. "I've been in politics thirty-five years and everything that could be said about a human being has been said about me. But my wife has never been in politics. She has always conducted herself in a circumspect manner and no one has a right to make derogatory remarks about her. Now your wife has said many unkind things about Mrs. Truman. And as long as I am in residence here, she'll not be a guest in the White House."

As far as Truman was concerned, the matter was settled.

A FATHER'S REACTION

The President was also very proud of Margaret's ease and acceptance of the attention she received. Although outgoing in public, Margaret was instilled with the level-headed Midwestern basics of her parents. Truman admired Margaret's courage in seeking a singing career after she had graduated from George Washington University in 1947. When she sang in a concert at Constitution Hall on December 5, 1950, a music critic wrote a scathing review which was published the following day in the *Washington Post*. After reading it, Harry Truman wrote the critic an equally scathing letter:

I have just read your lousy review. . . . You sound like a frustrated man that never made a success, an eight-ulcer man on a four-ulcer job, and all four ulcers working.

I never met you, but if I do you'll need a new nose and plenty of beefsteak and perhaps a supporter below.

When Truman's letter was made public, it caused quite a stir. Some said it wasn't an action befitting the office of the President. But mothers and fathers across the country understood and agreed with his right to respond in such a manner.

Years later during a television interview, Truman was asked if he had done anything while he was President that he wished he hadn't. Truman said that, considering the information he had had at the time and within the course of events, he couldn't think of anything he would have done differently except he probably wouldn't have written such a letter to "that critic." He added, however, that he thought, on occasion, even the President had the right to react like a father.

ENOUGH IS ENOUGH

The Korean War, the McCarthy witch hunts, and constant battles with a conservative Congress dominated President Truman's last years in the White House. For him, they were hard years and in many ways extremely disappointing.

His hopes for securing a medicare bill were dashed and he found having to constantly defend his actions was very taxing. Scandals involving other government officials annoyed and distressed him. Accusations that Harry Truman might have been involved in some of their shoddy deals infuriated him.

Despite the problems, most Democrats thought Truman would run again for reelection. But at a Jefferson-Jackson Day Dinner on March 29, 1952, the 5,300 guests were stunned when the President announced he would not seek another term in office. His announcement was no surprise to his family and close friends. Truman had made his decision four months earlier. He said that the job was a "man killer" and he didn't "want to be carried out of the White House in a pine box."

Some Democrats hoped Dwight David Eisenhower, one of the most respected generals of World War II, would be their candidate. But when Eisenhower decided to run on the Republican ticket, Truman picked Adlai Stevenson, the governor of Illinois, for the Democratic candidacy.

ADLAI STEVENSON II — Democratic nominee for the United States Presidency in 1952 and 1956. He was defeated both times by the Republican candidate, Dwight D. Eisenhower. Born in 1900 at Los Angeles, California, he was the grandson of Vice-President Adlai E. Stevenson who served in Grover Cleveland's administration. After finishing his studies at Princeton, Harvard, and Northwestern universities, he practiced law in Chicago. From 1933 to 1934, he held his first public office as special counsel to the Agricultural Adjustment Administration. During World War II, Stevenson assisted the Secretary of the Navy, Frank Knox, and then directed a United States mission on occupation policies in Italy. In 1948, he was elected governor of Illinois. His *Major Campaign Speeches* was published in 1952. He also authored *Call to Greatness* (1954) and *What I Think* (1956). In addition, Mr. Stevenson served as United States Permanent Representative to the United Nations until his death in 1965.

DWIGHT D. EISENHOWER — thirty-fourth President of the United States. Appointed Supreme Commander of the Allied Expeditionary Forces in Europe during the Second World War, he possessed the ability to bind together the feuding Allied military leaders into a state of mutual agreement and formed the most powerful combination of combat soldiers ever in existence. On June 6, 1944, he directed the successful D-Day invasion of Europe. This mammoth assault, code named "Operation Overlord," launched the largest amphibious landing in history by way of the Normandy beaches of France. Following the total triumph of the Allies in World War II, Eisenhower became Supreme Commander of the NATO Forces in Europe until 1952 when he received the Republican Party nomination for the United States Presidency. At the age of sixty-three, he became President, serving from 1953 until 1961. Retiring to a country home in Gettysburg, Pennsylvania, he died in 1969 at the age of seventy-nine.

TRUMAN vs. EISENHOWER

Although some voters considered Stevenson an intellectual with the vocabulary of a college professor, he ran an eloquent and admirable campaign. Since the Democrats had dominated the White House for twenty years and the general's popularity was immense, it is doubtful that anyone could have beaten Eisenhower. Even though Stevenson received considerably more votes than had been predicted, Eisenhower easily won the election.

During the campaign, Truman and Eisenhower were at odds with each other. Truman heard that during a speech Senator Joseph McCarthy insinuated that General George C. Marshall was a traitor. Eisenhower had stood by on the same speaking platform but had not come to the defense of his wartime comrade-at-arms. Truman publicly rebuked Eisenhower's lack of response. Never having been previously engaged in political campaigning, Eisenhower may have taken many of Truman's scathing comments personally.

The atmosphere between Truman and Eisenhower on Inauguration Day was chilly. Traditionally, the outgoing President always invited the incoming one for a pre-inaugural lunch at the White House. But Eisenhower did not accept Truman's invitation. And when the car arrived to pick up Truman for the inaugural ceremony, Eisenhower refused to greet the outgoing President as had always been the custom. Rather than hold up the ceremony, Truman stepped outside and got in the car. As they traveled to the Capitol Building, there was very little conversation between the two men.

Truman, a man who respected tradition, felt presidential protocol had been insulted. He privately vowed he would not speak to Eisenhower again until he apologized.

Following the inauguration, Truman and Eisenhower would not meet or speak to each other again until nine years later. In November of 1961, Eisenhower was scheduled to speak at a ceremony in Kansas City, Missouri. A delegation asked Truman if he would meet with Eisenhower and attend the function. Truman said he would not. He told them, however, that if Eisenhower would like to come to the Truman Library, he would be pleased to welcome him and show him through the facilities.

Eisenhower accepted the invitation and the meeting of the two past Presidents was cordial, even friendly. There was no indication that Eisenhower ever apologized to Truman nor that Truman any longer felt he should.

With Margaret.

PRIVATE CITIZEN — ALMOST

On the evening of Eisenhower's inauguration, the old presidential railroad car that had been used in Truman's famous Whistle-stop Campaign was connected to a westbound train. It silently waited at Washington, D.C.'s Union Station.

When Mr. and Mrs. Truman and their daughter Margaret arrived at the station, they were surprised to find that over nine thousand people had left the inauguration parade to come and say good-bye. As Harry Truman, retired public servant, stepped onto the familiar platform to speak, many people in the crowd wept.

"May I say to you that I appreciate this more than any meeting I have ever attended as President or Vice-President or Senator," he told them. "This is the greatest demonstration that any man could have, because I'm just Mr. Truman, private citizen now.

"This is the first time you have ever sent me home in a blaze of glory. I can't adequately express my appreciation for what you are doing. I'll never forget it if I live to be a hundred."

As he finished, the crowd spontaneously displayed their admiration and affection by singing "Auld Lang Syne." Soon the train pulled out of the station and headed west toward Independence, Missouri. Bess Truman would later say January 20, 1953, was the happiest day of her life because, at long last, the Harry S. Trumans were allowed to "go home."

Even in his retirement, Harry Truman was vigorous. As always, he started his day early, took his walk, read the newspapers, and wrote volumes of letters. In addition, he began writing his memoirs and spoke to students at numerous colleges and universities.

As a father, Truman had voiced his concern that Margaret might follow the pattern of many women in the Truman family and never marry. Margaret only laughed at such comments. She insisted she would marry but not while her father was President.

Three years after her father's retirement from office, on April 21, 1956, she proved her point. She and Clifton Daniel were married.

E. CLIFTON DANIEL, JR. – husband of Margaret Truman. He began as a reporter for the *New York Times* and later became its managing editor. After thirty-three years with the paper, he retired in October of 1977. He died on February 20, 2000 at the age of 87.

AWARDS AND CHALLENGES

Shortly after Margaret's marriage, Mr. and Mrs. Truman traveled to England and toured Europe. They were welcome visitors everywhere they went. The British and Europeans crowded the streets to see the designer of the Marshall Plan and the originator of the Truman Doctrine.

In England, the Trumans enjoyed a warm reunion with Sir Winston and Lady Churchill. Oxford University awarded the former President an honorary Doctor of Civil Law degree.

Harry and Bess Truman became grandparents when Margaret's first son, Clifton Truman Daniel, was born in 1957. Two years later, she presented them with another grandson, William Wallace Daniel. A third grandson, Harrison Gates Daniel, was born in 1963 and a fourth grandson, Thomas Washington Daniel, was born in 1966.

The designing and construction of the Truman Library and Museum in Independence, Missouri, was the largest project of Truman's retirement. The Library was built with donations from thousands of people. When the first section was completed, Mr. Truman presented to the Library over 3½ million pages of documents from his own presidential files. The main purpose of the Library, as Truman saw it, was to teach young and old alike the purpose of the President.

Mr. Truman maintained the President is six persons in one:
1. He is the executive officer of the government.
2. He is the leader of his party.
3. He has certain legislative duties consisting of initialing and signing bills or vetoing them.
4. He is the social head of the state.
5. He is the commander in chief of the armed forces.
6. He is the lobbyist for the people.

After the opening of the Library, Mr. Truman received visitors from all walks of life — presidents, statesmen, foreign dignitaries, entertainers, plumbers, steelworkers, secretaries, teachers, cab drivers, housewives, college students, and his favorites: school children of all ages.

TRUMAN LIBRARY — situated upon a hill facing U.S. Highway 24 in Independence, Missouri. The Truman Library was built of Indiana limestone and opened to the public in 1957.

With Mrs. Truman.

With President Kennedy.

JOHN F. KENNEDY — first Roman Catholic to become President of the United States. Born in Brookline, Massachusetts, he was a son of Joseph P. Kennedy, future ambassador to England. John Kennedy graduated from Harvard University with honors in 1940 and, shortly thereafter, served as a PT boat commander during World War II. His bravery in the fighting earned him a Purple Heart and the Navy and Marine Corps Medal for gallantry in battle. Following the end of the war, Kennedy began his political career in the Democratic Party. From 1947 to 1953, he represented Massachusetts in Congress, and in 1952, he became a U.S. Senator. As an author, Kennedy was awarded the Pulitzer biography prize for his *Profiles in Courage* written in 1956. In 1961, at the age of forty-three, he became the thirty-fifth President of the United States. An extremely popular leader, he possessed great wit, compassion, style, and handsome features. His presence in the White House, however, was brief for he was assassinated on November 22, 1963, while making an official visit to Dallas, Texas.

KENNEDY'S NEW FRONTIER

Even in retirement, Truman remained active as a Democratic firehorse; when the political bell rang, he was ready to go. He loved the political process and the excitement of an election.

Shortly before the 1960 campaign, a charming redheaded Irishman, John Fitzgerald Kennedy, called on Truman at the Library in Independence. Senator Kennedy was about to make his bid for the Democratic nomination and hoped to gain Truman's support. Before the meeting had ended, it was obvious that Truman wasn't going to give it. Truman had already decided to support Missouri Senator Stuart Symington.

But once Kennedy won the nomination, Truman gracefully accepted the fact and vigorously supported his campaign by making a series of speeches.

After Kennedy was elected, he displayed his gratitude by inviting the Trumans to the White House. Kennedy's gracious Irish manners and his open respect for Mr. and Mrs. Truman could not be resisted. Soon Truman grew genuinely fond of the new President.

Harry Truman was equally impressed with Jacqueline Kennedy's interest in restoring the White House that had been sadly neglected since the Truman years. In turn, she publicly and privately praised Mr. Truman's past contributions in having the building restored.

On November 19, 1961, President Truman attended the funeral of his colleague and longtime friend, Speaker of the House Sam Rayburn. During the services a very touching photograph was taken. To the right, seated side by side, were two past Presidents of the United States, Harry S. Truman and Dwight D. Eisenhower. To the far left sat the present President, John F. Kennedy, and next to him the future President, Lyndon Baines Johnson.

Two years later to the month in Dallas, Texas, as a motorcade moved through streets lined by thousands of cheering Texans, a sniper's bullets ended the life of John F. Kennedy. Truman joined the nation in mourning the death of the country's leader. He was personally saddened by the loss of a friend.

Truman said he believed that if John F. Kennedy had lived to complete another four years in office, he would have become one of the great Presidents.

During the last three years of Truman's life he experienced several health problems. On December 26, 1972, at the age of eighty-eight, Harry S. Truman died in Kansas City, Missouri's Research Hospital.

On the closing page of Margaret's book, *Harry S. Truman,* she quotes her father's terse comment in regard to how a President should conduct himself.

"Do your duty," he said, "and history will do you justice."

Even those persons who might not agree with President Truman's politics or all of the decisions he made would be hard-pressed not to agree that Harry S. Truman certainly did his duty as he saw it.

In the years since, history is already placing his name in the ranks as one of the great Presidents of the United States of America and as one of the greatest international leaders the world has ever known.

During a period of seven years, nine months, and eight days, Harry S. Truman, the thirty-third President of the United States, not only walked with the giants of the world — he led them.

A PROPHECY OR A SET OF GOALS?

When Harry Truman was in high school, he read *Locksley Hall* by Alfred Tennyson. He was so impressed, he made a copy and placed it in his wallet and always carried it with him.

In reading the verses today, it is easy to see that line by line the destiny of Harry S. Truman is clearly outlined — which poses two fascinating questions. When young Harry Truman read these lines, did he recognize a prophecy of his future? Or, by admiring those words and carrying them with him, were his goals altered and his destiny changed? These are the types of questions that challenge rational thinking and excite the imagination.

For I dipt into the future, far as human eye could see,
Saw the Vision of the world, and all the wonder that would be;
Saw the heavens fill with commerce, argosies of magic sails,
Pilots of the purple twilight, dropping down with costly bales;
Heard the heavens fill with shouting, and there rain'd a ghastly dew
From the nations' airy navies grappling in the central blue;
Far along the world-wide whisper of the south-wind rushing warm,
With the standards of the peoples plunging thro' the thunder-storm;
Till the war-drum throbb'd no longer, and the battleflags were furl'd
In the Parliament of Man, the Federation of the World.
There the common sense of most shall hold a fretful realm in awe,
And the kindly earth shall slumber, lapt in universal law.

THE VERY QUOTABLE
MR. TRUMAN

Harry Truman was a creative dresser. He had suits, shirts, and hats for every occasion. In his position as President, the variety of styles and selections he chose were both proper and surprising.

When he was at work, he wore well tailored suits and tastefully selected ties, but when he and his family vacationed in Key West, Florida, or on the presidential yacht, out came the wildly patterned and brightly colored shirts.

A proponent of physical fitness, the President enjoyed his morning walks. He loved to swim and bowl and routinely exercised.

Reporters liked his quick wit and ever ready quips because they always made colorful copy. His straightforward manner of speaking was something new in a politician. He had a great sense of timing and could spit out a oneliner in a style that challenged the most polished delivery of the best stand-up comedian.

With his folksy rhetoric, he often pricked the pompous bubbles of other politicians. Many of his off-the-cuff statements are as humorous now as they were the day he said them. And his observations still have the power to stimulate our thinking.

HARRY S. TRUMAN COMMENTS ABOUT:

The Presidency

"The President of the United States represents 154,000,000 people. Most of them have no lobby and no special representation. The President must represent all the people.

"Therefore, the President must be a sort of super-public relations man. His powers are great, but he must know how to make people get along together. His ceremonial duties which are incidental to his official duties are all part of his public relations duties.

"Today the responsibility of the President is greater than ever. The President has to know what takes place all around the world. He has to have all sorts of world contacts. Because today we are, whether we like it or not, the most powerful nation in the world.

"Our government cannot function properly unless the President is master in his own house and unless the executive departments and agencies of the government, including the armed forces, are responsible only to the President."

"No President ever can tell what the best approach to world affairs is. He has to use his best judgment and try to keep things on an even keel for the welfare of his own country. Any schoolboy can tell him what he should have done, after the fact is accomplished."

"The President is responsible for the administration of his office. And that means for the administration of the entire executive branch. It is not the business of Congress to run the agencies of government for the President."

Presidents He Admired

"The Presidents I admire most are George Washington, because of his ability to set up a government; Thomas Jefferson, who aroused the American people to take an interest in their government; and Andrew Jackson, because he carried out his policies despite all the opposition they made for him. For the beginning history of our country, those three are the great Presidents of that time.

"Jefferson, I think, is the greatest ethical teacher of our time. He was unusual in that he was able, as Governor of Virginia, member of the Continental Congress and President of the United States, to put his teachings into practice.

"Of course, Lincoln came along and saved the Union. If we hadn't had a man of decision there, at that time, the country would have broken up into four or five small republics which never would have had a place in the world. Conditions then had to be met by a man like Abraham Lincoln who knew where he was going and why.

"The next President who really made an impression on me was Grover Cleveland. From 1885 to 1889, he did some wonderful things during that period. The next man who really made an impact upon the government of the United States was Theodore Roosevelt. He was the one who got after the financial pirates of the country. Following him, of course, was Franklin Delano Roosevelt. . . . He will be present in the galaxy of the great Presidents of the United States.

"Woodrow Wilson is one of the most important of the Presidents. He had written a history of the Presidency previous to his entering office. He used his knowledge of how the President should run the government. In his first term, he got through some of the best legislation ever put on the books of the U.S. Government. Had it not been that we fell into the First World War, his whole administration would have been one of growth and progress. His designing of the League of Nations, and his earnest efforts to have it and other good programs included in the Treaty of Versailles, killed him in the long run. He was one of the great Presidents along with the others which I have named."

"Some of the Presidents were great and some of them weren't. I can say that, because I wasn't one of the great Presidents, but I had a good time trying to be one, I can tell you that."

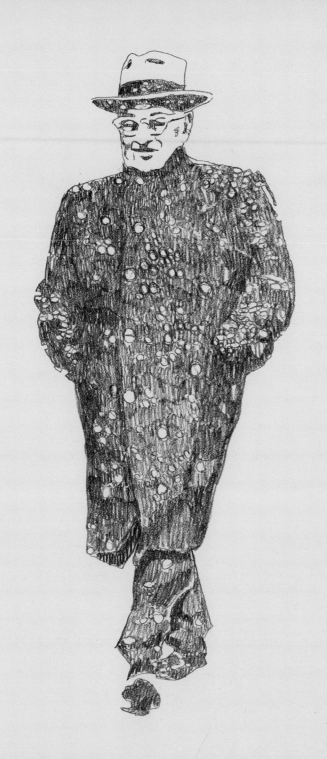

Military Men as Presidents

"They're honorable men. They want to do the right thing, but they've been educated in a manner that's like a horse with blinders on— he sees only one direction right down the road."

Military Opinion of Presidents

"Some of the generals and the admirals and the career men in government look upon the occupant of the White House as only a temporary nuisance who soon will be succeeded by another temporary occupant who won't find out what it is all about for a long time and then it will be too late to do anything about it."

America's Destiny

"America hasn't even begun to imagine its great destiny."

"The role of the United States is the leadership of the free world. It is and it always will be. There's a spiritual force behind the United States that helps it lead the free world. We did something after the Second World War that no other country in history has ever done— we rehabilitated our enemies. You won't find that in history anywhere."

"No nation on this globe should be more internationally minded than America because it was built by all nations."

Making Decisions

"The exertions, troubles and decisions of the Presidency weigh on a greater scale than you'll find anywhere else. I've tried to handle them all the same way. I slept well, walked all the time when I had the opportunity— a mile, mile and a half, sometimes two. When the time came to meet the business of the Presidency, I was ready for it. I managed it the best way I could. I got the best information I could possibly get and then I made the decision. I never worried about it at all— I never looked back. The decision was made."

"If you're lucky and can get somebody who can make decisions in places of importance, especially in politics, things always run much better."

"It's always been my opinion that the people who can make decisions, in the business world and anywhere else, are the ones who make it to the top."

Government

"I think our Constitution and its Bill of Rights is the greatest document of government in the history of the world and I am doing my best to contribute my share to upholding it."

"No government is perfect. One of the chief virtues of a democracy, however, is that its defects are always visible and under democratic processes can be pointed out and corrected."

"If you want an efficient government, why then go someplace where they have a dictatorship and you'll get it."

"I can't go along with the setting-up of a supergovernment outside the control of both the Congress and the President no matter what good purpose it may serve."

"Efficiency alone is not enough in government . . . .

"Hitler learned that efficiency without justice is a vain thing."

History

"There is nothing new in the world except the history you do not know."

"I had no trouble sleeping . . . . I read myself to sleep every night in the White House, reading a biography on the troubles of some President in the past."

War and Peace

"Peace is the goal of my life. I'd rather have lasting peace in the world than be President. I wish for peace, I work for peace and I pray for peace continually."

"It all seems to have been in vain. Memories are short and appetites for power and glory are insatiable. Old tyrants depart. New ones take their place. Old allies become the foe. The recent enemy becomes the friend. It is all very baffling and trying, but we cannot lose hope, we cannot despair. For it is all too obvious that if we do not abolish war on this earth, then surely, one day, war will abolish us from the earth."

Patriotism

"I have said many a time that I think the Un-American Activities Committee in the House of Representatives was the most un-American thing in America."

"I think a test oath for students is silly. Teachers who don't know enough to teach you about our great government have no business being teachers, and after you've learned all you can about it, if you become one who doesn't appreciate his government, you are welcome to go to Russia or somewhere else, and then you can satisfy yourself."

Politics

"One rule that I did make in the beginning in politics was that I would have nothing to do with money. I just wouldn't handle it. I wouldn't collect it, I wouldn't distribute it, I wouldn't have anything in the world to do with it. And the boss politicians respected me because of this, although they never did understand it."

"I never ran for a political office I wanted. But I've fought for every one I've ever had. Damn it! I've never had an office I didn't have to fight for, tooth and nail."

"I'm content just where I am. I'm happy in the Senate. I have friends and I don't have any political ambitions. You know, people call me a politician, and you know the way some say it. Well, you've got to be a politician in the first place to get to be a senator. When you're dead, they call you a statesman . . . ."

"Some Senators and Congressmen come in and pass the time of day, and then go out and help me save the world in the press."

"With such a record, how in heaven's name can the Republican Party claim credit for the farm program today? It reminds me of the flea that was on the back of a donkey crossing a bridge. When they got across, the flea said to the donkey, 'Boy, we sure did shake that bridge, didn't we!'"

"You don't get any double-talking from me. I'm either for something or against it, and you know it. You know what I stand for."

Elections

"I've been in many and many election campaigns as you people here in Missouri know. After the election's over, I bear no malice or feel badly toward anyone because the fellow who lost feels badly enough without eating crow."

"In 1946, two-thirds of you stayed home and didn't vote. We got that awful Eightieth Congress as a result. And you got just what you deserved because you didn't exercise your rights!"

"I don't care what your politics are, I don't care what you believe politically, and I don't care what your religion is, as long as you live by it and act by it. But you must watch out for those people who make mountains out of something that doesn't exist — not even a molehill! . . . The best way to handle them is to ridicule them. You know, there's no stuffed shirt that can stand ridicule. When you stick a pin in that stuffed shirt and let the wind out, he's through!"

"By their votes ye shall know them."

Public Opinion Polls

"Polls are like sleeping pills designed to lull the voters into sleeping on election day. You might call them sleeping polls.

"Some people think that public relations should be based on polls. That is nonsense.

"I wonder how far Moses would have gone if he had taken a poll in Egypt?

"What would Jesus Christ have preached if He had taken a poll in the land of Israel?

"Where would the Reformation have gone if Martin Luther had taken a poll?

"It isn't polls or public opinion alone of the moment that counts. It is right and wrong, and leadership — men with fortitude, honesty and a belief in the right that make epochs in the history of the world.

Freedom

"In the cause of freedom, we have to battle for the rights of people with whom we do not agree; and whom, in many cases, we may not like. These people test the strength of the freedoms which protect all of us. If we do not defend their rights, we endanger our own."

"People everywhere express themselves and live their own lives in terms of their own background and culture, and that is their God-given right, as long as they do not attempt to impose by force or intrigue their ideas on their neighbors.

"We in America have waged many bitter struggles to preserve our freedom.

"This freedom has enabled our masses of people to enjoy an ever improved standard of living, free from the kind of toil that still is breaking the backs of hundreds of millions of people. I would offer American experience, American skill, and American science to help lift the load from these people's backs. Many people who still live in the feudal ages are being hoodwinked by devilish propaganda today into false paradises."

Civil Rights

"We can't be leaders of the free world and draw a color line on opportunity."

The United Nations

"If nations could get together and discuss difficulties and deal in a fair manner with each other, there would never be a necessity for war."

"I think the United Nations has made great progress. It will take a long time to make it an ideal organization. The Constitution of the United States was a long time in being implemented. In fact, we had to fight ourselves before we found out how exactly to make it work. The United Nations may never be an ideal organization. But it's an organization that can maintain the peace of the world if it's properly supported."

"The human race has been striving for peace ever since civilization started. The United Nations represents the greatest organized attempt in the history of men to solve their differences without war."

Making Speeches

"I heard a fellow tell a story about how he felt when he had to make speeches. He said when he had to make a speech, he felt like the fellow who was at the funeral of his wife, and the undertaker had asked him if he would ride down to the cemetery in the same car with his mother-in-law. He said, 'Well, I can do it, but it's just going to spoil the whole day for me.'"

Truman, a critic of his own speeches, said of one:

"Seems to have made a hit according to all the papers. Shows you never can tell. I thought it was rotten."

While Truman was making a speech at a train station in Barstow, California, a woman yelled out: *"President Truman, you sound as if you have a cold."*

"That's because I ride around with my mouth open," the President quipped back.

"As you know, I speak plainly sometimes — in fact, I speak bluntly sometimes and I am going to speak plainly and bluntly today."

". . . If I keep you standing here in this rain any longer you will be against anything I want, and I wouldn't blame you. But I understand that you need the rain worse than you need to listen to any Presidential speech."

"I'm not going to demagogue until I have something to demagogue about."

Critics

"As always, I am just trying to do the job I am supposed to do, and a lot of times, in public service, that is an unusual procedure, so it causes comment."

"I am sometimes accused of claiming credit for every good thing that happened in the United States while I have been President, and, by the same token, accused of never admitting a mistake.

"As for the mistakes, I know that I make them like everybody else does, and I do admit them from time to time. However, it has not seemed necessary for me to spend a great deal of time calling attention to my mistakes because there have always been plenty of people who were willing to do that for me."

"I shall continue to do what I think is right whether anybody likes it or not."

Religion

"My Grandfather Young belonged to no church, but he supported many of them—Baptist, Methodist, Campbellite, and Presbyterian. They all met in the old church out in front of the house on the family farm on Sunday."

"I wish God Almighty would give the Children of Israel an Isaiah, the Christians a St. Paul, and the Sons of Ishmael a peep at the Golden Rule."

"I rather think there is an immense shortage of Christian charity among so-called Christians."

Atomic Energy

"Think what can be done, once our capital, our skills, our science— most of all, atomic energy— can be released from the tasks of defense and turned wholly to peaceful purposes around the world.

"There is no end to what can be done. I can't help but dream out loud a little here.

"The Tigris and Euphrates Valley can be made to bloom as it did in the times of Babylon and Nineveh. Israel can be made the country of milk and honey as it was in the time of Joshua. There is a plateau in Ethiopia. . . . Enough food can be raised to feed a hundred million people. There are places in South America— places like Colombia and Venezuela and Brazil— just like that plateau in Ethiopia— places where food could be raised for millions of people.

"These things can be done, and they are self-liquidating projects. If we can get peace and safety in the world under the United Nations, the developments will come so fast we will not recognize the world in which we now live."

"I believe that atomic energy should not be used to fatten the profits of big business. I believe that it should be used to benefit all the people.

"The largest private corporation in the world is far too small to be entrusted with such power, least of all for its own profit."

The Press

"Whenever the press quits abusing me, I know I'm in the wrong pew."

"Editors are peculiar animals— they throw mud and bricks at you the whole year round— then they make one favorable statement which happens to agree with facts and they think they should be hugged and kissed for it."

"... There are a great many instances where editorials are mailed to me from out of town .... I get up before daylight every morning— I have the reveille habit— and I spend a good part of that time going over all the Washington papers and the New York papers, Baltimore Sun, Philadelphia Bulletin, and many others that I have time to read. But I read them myself because I like to read them.

"And I find out lots of things about myself that I never heard of."

"I'm amazed sometimes when I find that some of you disagree with me. When I consider how you disagree among yourselves, I'm somewhat comforted. I'll begin to think that maybe I'm all right anyway."

"If they want to ask me some impudent questions, I'll try to give them some impudent answers."

A reporter once asked President Truman if it was as windy in Independence as it was in Washington. Truman replied: "It is when I'm there."

Television Communication

"The television can be used in the proper education of the people by informing them on how the country and the rest of the world stands and be able to meet any situation which may come up."

"Television is a tremendous influence because it can give you information about an event as it happens and as it looks."

"Radio, along with television, is the greatest system of communication in the history of the world and every president, since that has been the case, should make use of it."

Morals

"There's a vast majority of people in the United States who are just as moral as people can be. The moral fiber of a country that is free is higher than that of other countries which are not free."

"Privileges and rights are sometimes taken for granted. A good jolt now and then is just what it takes to put them to work again."

The Morals of Government

"A moral code is one based on proper relations with other people and on a faith in the religious concept of a future after the life on earth.

"Egypt, Mesopotamia, Greece, Rome all had such moral codes.

"Ours comes from ancient Israel and the Sermon on the Mount.

"Great teachers like Moses, Isaiah, Confucius, Buddha, Mohammed, Saint Thomas Aquinas, Martin Luther, John Knox and many others were imbued with honor, truth and justice.

"The basis of all great moral codes is 'Do to and for others what you would have others do to and for yourself.'

"In ancient times, Jesus Christ was the greatest teacher of them all—not only ancient but modern."

Music

On the "Missouri Waltz":

> *It's a ragtime song and if you let me say what I think, I don't give a damn about it, but I can't say it out loud because it's the song of Missouri. It's as bad as "The Star Spangled Banner" as far as music is concerned.*

Truman's sometimes informal manner surprised Washington society. Once, while playing for a gathering of Methodist ladies, he winked as he told them:
> *"When I played this, Stalin signed the Potsdam Agreement."*

"If I hadn't been President of the United States, I probably would have ended up as a piano player in a bawdy house."

Education

"When you get an education, that is something nobody can take from you—money is only temporary—but what you have in your head, if you have the right kind of head, stays with you."

"I've always been sorry I did not get a university education in the regular way. But I got it in the Army the hard way—and it stuck."

"The best weapon against totalitarianism and communism is the education of youngsters. If they're properly educated, as they seem to be in this free country, then we'll go forward. And unless we can go forward as a free nation, there's no progress."

"Next to the mother and father in the home, the school teacher is one of the most important people in this country. Paid less than a laborer."

"There are a great number of teachers who are dedicated enough to do the job regardless of pay. For that very reason, they should be treated as the rest of the population is treated and put in the financial scale they belong in."

Young People

"Students in the United States are the finest in the world. They ask the most intelligent questions. They're after information. You should look them in the face. They're the finest people in the world. They're the citizens coming on."

"I don't want to talk about the juvenile delinquency. There isn't any more of it in proportion to the population than when I grew up—only we could cover it up. There wasn't as much reporting about it as there is now."

"How to make a contribution to the government, that's what's in the minds of most of these youngsters. The vast majority are trying to find out how the U.S. Government runs in relation to the President."

"I would like young people to find out what they have and what they have to do to keep it. And in order to do that, they must be given some idea of what the government is and how it works from one end of Pennsylvania Avenue to the other.

"I would like very much for youngsters to know that they didn't obtain these things for nothing and without effort. Also, they must know that they can't keep them without the same effort put forth by them and their generation as has been put forth by generations before them."

"Young people are trying to find some way to put things in order to help the United States go on in a prosperous manner. I think they're going to do it."

"The totalitarian state has not made much of an impression on young people. Some kids have foolish ideas but, in the long run, those youngsters will come out all right. I'm not worried about them at all. The important thing is to get the information to them in a manner which they can understand the government and how it works."

"'Youth, the Hope of the World.' That was the motto on the high school front door from which I graduated, only it was written— 'Juventus Spes Mundi.'"

The White House

"I have collected since I have been in the White House a great many stories about the improvement of that structure and about the various Presidents and First Ladies who have been in it.

"There's a story around the White House that Mrs. Millard Fillmore brought the first bathtub into the White House. There is also a story in connection with it, that the local medical association in Cincinnati, Ohio, passed a resolution calling Mrs. Fillmore an indecent person because she had put a bathtub in the White House.

"This medical association in Cincinnati said that it was unsanitary, that it was unhealthy, that no person should take all his clothes off at one time.

"Well, my friends, there has been some progress since that date, and I want to say to you, there are more bathtubs in the White House now than there are in the Benjamin Franklin Hotel."

"The White House is the center of all the limelight in the country. It's extremely difficult for the Presidential family to live normally. There's always someone trying to find a way into the White House to see you. My mother and sister lived in Grandview, Missouri, and there was always someone wanting to use them to get what they wanted from me."

His Family

John Anderson Truman:

"My father was a very energetic person. He worked from daylight to dark, all the time. And his code was honesty and integrity. His word was good. When he told us that something was a fact with regard to a horse or a cow or a piece of land, that was just what it was. It was the truth. And he raised my brother and myself to put honor above profit. He was quite a man, my dad was. He was not a talker. He was a doer. He lived what he believed, and taught the rest of us to do the same thing."

"My father was not a failure. After all, he was the father of a President of the United States."

Martha Ellen Young Truman:

"My mother taught us the moral code and started us in Sunday school. She was always interested in our school programs, and our place was always the gathering place for all the kids in the neighborhood because my mother liked children and liked to see them have a good time, and liked to help them have a good time. She taught us the right thing to do and made us do it.

"One of the funniest things she said when I brought her to Washington in the plane and got her off at the airport and all the photographers and newsmen crowded around her was, 'Oh, fiddlesticks, why didn't you tell me about this, and I would have stayed home.'"

Bess Truman:

"She was my first sweetheart," Truman said many years later. *"Her eyes are still blue, but her hair is not golden—it's silver, like mine. And she is still my sweetheart."*

"When we first moved to Independence, my mother took us to Sunday school at the Presbyterian Church. I was six years old. In my Sunday school class was a beautiful girl with golden curls. I was smitten at once and still am—she's Mrs. Truman and the mother of the loveliest daughter in the world."

"Whenever a controversial subject came up, I'd usually consult Bess because she has a pretty good idea of what the everyday person is thinking and would do under the circumstances."

Margaret Truman:

When asked about his daughter's active interest in photography in the White House, President Truman commented:
> *"It's not enough that my homely countenance is at the mercy of the press—I have to have a photographer in the family."*

> *"We ought to have been a vaudeville team. We would have had lots of fun. Margaret could have sung and Mrs. Truman could have managed the act."*

Missouri

> *"Now Missouri has had a number of notorious characters. The three, I guess, most notorious are Mark Twain, Jesse James, and me. Mark and Jesse are dead and I have to fill in for them, so here I am."*

Truman loved quoting Mark Twain's comment:
> *"If we had less statesmanship, we could get along with fewer battleships"; and another favorite was, "Always be good. This will gratify some people and astonish the rest."*

> *"I wonder if it may not be such simple characters as Tom Sawyer and Huckleberry Finn who will, as symbols, show the world our undying contribution to the civilization on our continent . . . ."*

Independence, Missouri

> *"I've got the same friends and neighbors I've had all my life. Independence is a wonderful place to live. Finest town in the world. I've been in nearly every town in the United States and a great many foreign cities. I wouldn't give up Independence for the whole city of New York even if you threw in Brooklyn."*

> *"If a president can go back with the people proud of him, of course, he can go back to his roots. They have to remember that's where he came from. His friends and neighbors expect him to remember that's where he came from."*

> *"I like to stop and talk with people. I like to know what's going on in the town and understand what my neighbors are doing. I have a good time. In Independence, I usually walk when it's too early for many people to be out— about six or six-thirty. It's not done to avoid anyone but to be able to get in a good day's work."*

The Goals of the Truman Library

"I'm hoping to make it the study center of the executive branch of the government and to make available a fair historic account of every President. It's going to take a while but we've started collecting documents of all the Presidents in order to have a documented history of each one.

"Sam Rayburn, the Speaker of the House, has established a library in Texas which has copies of every bill that ever became a law from the beginning of the Continental Congress to this date. That library is for the study of the legislative branch of the government which is just as important as the executive. And when you put the two together, you have the history of the country from the operational end."

"I want to leave a record so the people will not have any difficulty in finding out what the President is up against when he's trying to make decision. This record will leave no doubt as to what the situation was and why it happened."

Awards

After being given the Freedom House Award:
> *You don't know how overcome I am. You don't know how difficult it is to be present at your own funeral and still be able to walk around.*

After being presented with a "grand champion" blue ribbon at a junior livestock show:
> *I don't know whether I'm the prize pig or what.*

Fame

"Men often mistake notoriety for fame, and would rather be remarked for their vices and follies than not be noticed at all!"

Walking

"When a man is over thirty-five, about the only exercise that does him any good is a good walk. The reason why that is so is because it affects every muscle in the body."

Hunting

"I do not believe in shooting at anything that cannot shoot back."

Common Sense

"There is nothing in the world that a boy couldn't have if he'd just have a teaspoonful of common sense."

"My favorite animal is the mule. He has more sense than a horse. He knows when to stop eating— and when to stop working."

Health

"If I felt any better, I couldn't stand it."

Income

"I am trying to fix it so the people in the middle-income bracket can live as long as the very rich and very poor . . . ."

His Salty Language

"Anybody who has been raised in the Midwest part of the United States has a strong vocabulary. And when the time comes, you just stand up and use it. There's nothing wrong with it. It's not intended to be profanity. It's to emphasize the conversation."

". . . I never gave them hell. It seemed like hell because I told the truth and they didn't."

How He Would Like History To See Him

". . . There is an epitaph in Boothill Cemetery in Tombstone, Arizona, which reads, 'Here lies Jack Williams; he done his damndest.' What more can a person do?"

INDEX

HARRY S. TRUMAN
THE MAN WHO WALKED WITH GIANTS
designed, written & illustrated
by
David Melton
Published by
Richardson Printing -- (Special Edition)
Independence Press -- (First Edition Hardback)

MANUSCRIPT
Footnotes, biographies & index
Teresa M. Melton-Symon

EDITORS
Evelyn Maples
Nancy Melton

RESEARCH
Teresa M. Melton-Symon

PRINT PROJECT MANAGER
John McFatrich

FILM COMPOSITION
Jerry Gregory
Rob Price
Thad Parnell

PRINT PRODUCTION
Plant Superintendent
David Barker

Estimator/Production Coordinator
Buddy Barker

Pressmen
Rick Edmondson
Jeff Bycraft
Jeff Smith
Jimmy Proctor
Eric Smith
Roberto Lozano

We thank the Staff of the Harry S. Truman Library Institute for their co-operation and enthusiasm for this special 30th Anniversary edition – most notably, Michael Devine – Director, Alex Burden – Executive Vice-President and Kim Rausch – Development Coordinator. We especially are grateful to the financial support and devotion to this book of:

THE NORMAN & ELAINE POLSKY FAMILY SUPPORTING FOUNDATION WITHIN THE GREATER KANSAS CITY COMMUNITY FOUNDATION AND WITH THE JOHNSON COUNTY COMMUNITY COLLEGE FOUNDATION

DAVID MELTON
– Author & Illustrator

David Melton, who passed away in 2002, was one of the most versatile and prolific talents on the literary and art scenes. His credits seem to describe the creative efforts of several people.

Mr. Melton's literary works span the gamut of factual prose, analytical essays, news reporting, magazine articles, features, short stories and poetry and novels in both the adult and juvenile fields. Over the years, seventeen of his books have been published – many of which have been international bestsellers.

His first book, TODD, a personal account of the Meltons' search for educational and medical help for their brain-injured child, is considered a classic in its genre. His other parent/child-oriented books have received critical acclaim for thorough research and

(Continued)

presentation of information and, most importantly, have affected the lives of thousands of parents and children.

His first novel, THEODORE, for which Mr. Melton was presented The Thorpe Menn Award for literary excellence in 1978, received outstanding reviews. Film rights for THEODORE are currently held by Twentieth Century-Fox Studios.

Mr. Melton also developed a reputation as an illustrator and graphics designer. Aside from illustrating several books – some his own – many of his paintings and drawings have been reproduced in numerous countries as posters, puzzles, calendars, book jackets, record covers and other books. Original works have been exhibited in the Harry S. Truman Presidential Library & Museum, the National Headquarters Building of the Medicare Bureau in Baltimore, Maryland, The Institutes for the Achievement of Human Potential in Philadelphia, PA, Notre Dame University and in many colleges and universities throughout the country.

Mr. Melton was a guest speaker to hundreds of professional, social, civic and educational institutions and has been interviewed on both national television and radio programs.

Mr. Melton lived in the Kansas City Metropolitan area with his wife, Nancy, and their two children, Todd and Teresa (Traci).

For their exemplary work with their own son and for affecting the lives of so many parents and children in positive ways throughout the world by their books, magazine articles and public speaking, in May of 1978, the Meltons were presented The Benjamin Franklin Freedom Award. His daughter, Teresa (Traci) Marguerite Melton-Symon continues to carry on his legacy by lecturing and bringing forward his company, Landmark House, Ltd. and the annual National Kids-in-Print Contest for Students.

OTHER BOOKS BY DAVID MELTON
(Partial List)

Author:

TODD
Prentice Hall – United States
Leslie Frewen Publishers, Ltd. – Great Britain
Hyperian-Verlag – Germany
Armando Armando – Italy

A BOY CALLED HOPELESS
Independence Press

THEODORE
Independence Press

SURVIVAL KIT FOR THE PARENTS OF TEENAGERS
St. Martin's Press

WRITTEN & ILLUSTRATED BY...
Landmark House, Ltd.

HOW TO WRITE A BOOK IN 40 DAYS
Landmark House, Ltd.

Author & Illustrator:

I'LL SHOW YOU THE MORNING SUN
Stanyon-Random House

JUDY GARLAND – A REMEMBRANCE
Stanyon –Random House

THE ONE & ONLY AUTOBIOGRAPHY OF RALPH MILLER
(The Dog Who Thought He Was a Boy)
Independence Press

Illustrator:

WHAT TO DO ABOUT YOUR BRAIN-INJURED CHILD
By: Glenn Doman
Doubleday

IMAGES OF GREATNESS
Independence Press – Images of Greatness Commission

EMOTIONAL IMPACT SERIES
(Books 2 through 7)
By: Dr. Adolph Moser
Landmark House, Ltd.